P9-CLC-900

Praise for *Cultivating a Culture of Learning*

"*Cultivating a Culture of Learning* is a profound and crucial wake-up call in the field of education. A collection of brilliant insights—contemporary and historical—into the need for mind-body-spirit balance and how to accomplish that in today's varied teaching environments. These educators value 'process over product,' a real coup in a world that needs more authenticity. This is precisely the sort of revamping our educational systems need!" —Chris Saade, author of *Second Wave Spirituality: Passion for Peace, Passion for Justice*

"As a recently retired education professor, I am delighted Kathryn Byrnes, Jane E. Dalton, and Elizabeth Hope Dorman are curating this series of books on contemplative teacher education. Several years ago, a student interested in contemplative education, but frustrated with the lack of specific examples, said to me, 'I get what you are saying, but I have no idea how to teach that way.' Colleagues who may feel uncertain about 'stepping into the unknown' in their teaching, who prefer to plan lessons to eliminate uncertainty, will benefit from the theory of practice presented in this text. The essential understandings and practical models shared engage both teacher educators and students of teaching in deepening their understanding of contemplative teaching and learning."—Tom Bassarear, retired professor of education, Keene State College

"Kathryn Byrnes, Jane E. Dalton, and Elizabeth Hope Dorman are to be commended for this vitally required three-volume series for the field of contemplative education. The series offers abundant riches in theory, application, and research for teacher education.

It is widely understood, if not applied, that if schools are to avoid becoming increasingly irrelevant and ineffective in an age of distraction, anxiety, and superficiality, then how we educate educators has to change. At a time where, on a global scale, radical changes in K–12 curricula are occurring, these volumes are indeed welcome. Doubling down on instructional strategies, e-learning devices, and content expertise miss the point entirely: we need to attend to the inner lives of aspiring teachers so they in turn can foster a learning environment that honors both the interior and exterior world of students.

The three-volume work edited by Byrnes, Dalton, and Dorman fills a timely need to apply the principles and processes of contemplative inquiry to preservice teacher education. Today's teacher education needs to include contemplative orientations to address the challenges of preservice teachers becoming more fully human and to offer specific contemplative foundations and approaches for those who design and teach in preservice programs. The essays in these volumes will be valuable to both faculty and the preservice teachers themselves.

Drawing from a rich and eclectic range of teacher education programs infused with various contemplative practices, the first volume, *Cultivating a Culture of Learning: Contemplative Practice, Pedagogy, and Research in Education*, serves as an extremely useful primer. The editors and contributors outline the many benefits contemplative orientations and pedagogies offer, reminding us that teaching and learning 'at its best is one of the most elemental of human exchanges,' one that requires 'all dimensions of human awareness and action.' Contemplative approaches allow us to deepen the inquiry into self, self-with-other, and self-with-the-world, and the contributors in this first volume offer a truly rich banquet of insight, depth, and practical pedagogical and curricular suggestions. They cover theory, practices, and research into the application of contemplative inquiry in teacher education, and they write from firsthand experience. Importantly, the chapters in this book advocate for creating spaces where the inner life is nurtured and plumbed, allowing intuition, creativity, and heart-centered learning to flourish.

The examples of preservice training initiatives outlined in volume one, while different in pedagogical approach, share a common commitment to illuminating and developing the inner lives of students. By providing such an illustrative array of program examples, the editors demonstrate that there are many paths to the same destination.

Perhaps the greatest contribution in this book by Byrnes, Dalton, and Dorman is the recognition that the inner lives of teachers and their students are neither incidental nor insignificant, but rather essential ingredients in engaged, dynamic teaching and sustained deep learning. This volume is timely and needed on its own and generates positive anticipation about the two volumes yet to come."—Heesoon Bai, Laurie Anderson, and Charles Scott, program coordinators of Master of Education in Contemplative Inquiry and Approaches to Education, Simon Fraser University, Canada

Cultivating a Culture of Learning

Cultivating a Culture of Learning

Contemplative Practices, Pedagogy, and Research in Education

Edited by
Kathryn Byrnes
Jane E. Dalton
Elizabeth Hope Dorman

ROWMAN & LITTLEFIELD
Lanham • Boulder • New York • London

Published by Rowman & Littlefield
A wholly owned subsidiary of The Rowman & Littlefield Publishing Group, Inc.
4501 Forbes Boulevard, Suite 200, Lanham, Maryland 20706
www.rowman.com

Unit A, Whitacre Mews, 26-34 Stannary Street, London SE11 4AB

Copyright © 2018 by Kathryn Byrnes, Jane E. Dalton, and Elizabeth Hope Dorman

All rights reserved. No part of this book may be reproduced in any form or by any electronic or mechanical means, including information storage and retrieval systems, without written permission from the publisher, except by a reviewer who may quote passages in a review.

British Library Cataloguing in Publication Information Available

Library of Congress Cataloging-in-Publication Data Available

ISBN 978-1-4758-3628-8 (hardback : alk. paper) | ISBN 978-1-4758-3629-5 (pbk. : alk. paper) |
    ISBN 978-1-4758-3630-1 (ebook)

♾ ™ The paper used in this publication meets the minimum requirements of American National Standard for Information Sciences Permanence of Paper for Printed Library Materials, ANSI/NISO Z39.48-1992.

Printed in the United States of America

Contents

Foreword

Laura I. Rendón

It never fails. When I address educators and ask them to identify the one or two key competencies that are absolutely essential for students to learn when they graduate from college, we generate two lists, depicting both intellectual and inner aptitudes. The longest competency list that emerges relates to inner-life skills, for example, being authentic, having integrity, working well with others, having a sense of meaning and purpose, seeing the glass half full, practicing presence, developing wisdom, having self-awareness, practicing empathy, seeking justice, and being open to new ideas.

And when I follow up and ask them how much time they spend developing exactly what they consider to be the most important competencies students should have learned when they leave college, there is an awkward silence and sometimes nervous laughter as educators realize that most of what they have done is to focus on traditional measures of learning related to cognitive development.

This simple exercise exemplifies that we are out of balance in education, and it is time to address this imbalance with a newly fashioned paradigm that appreciates and fosters not only intellectual development but also abilities that allow an individual to access inner knowing related to emotions, intuition, and wisdom.

Not only are we out of balance, but also this is a challenging, complex time when the demands of the teaching profession have become quite overwhelming, necessitating a new perspective that focuses on what and how to teach, as well as on the teacher whose role it is to construct and facilitate a pedagogy of wholeness. There is little professional development training for teachers to work with a pedagogy of wholeness that includes contemplative practices.

To that end, Kathryn Byrnes, Jane E. Dalton, and Elizabeth Hope Dorman have edited a collective trio of books providing invigorating, innovative ways that contemplative pedagogy can deepen the work of teaching and learning in today's P–12 classrooms. What the authors theorize is that contemplative pedagogy that focuses on deep learning experiences and reflective practices can strengthen teaching and learning, while supporting and enhancing teacher development. As suggested by David Hawkins (2007), each of the three books complement each other and are arranged to cover three important aspects of meaningful learning experiences.

The first book, *Cultivating a Culture of Learning: Contemplative Practices, Pedagogy, and Research in Education*, attends to the content of teaching, with examples of how to integrate contemplative practices in teacher education courses and programs.

The second book, *Impacting Teaching and Learning: Contemplative Practices, Pedagogy, and Research in Education*, addresses the who that is being taught and features current research on the impacts of contemplative practices and pedagogy in teacher education.

The third book, *The Teaching Self: Contemplative Practices, Pedagogy, and Research in Education*, focuses on who is doing the teaching, with a focus on the teaching self.

Collectively, these three books are representative of what I call sentipensante (sensing/thinking) pedagogy (Rendón, 2009). A sensing/thinking pedagogy is one that disrupts the entrenched notion that education should focus mainly, if not solely, on developing intellectual abilities such as critical thinking and problem solving.

As in sentipensante pedagogy, a more spacious view of education is offered in these three books, one that connects and places into balance outer knowing (intellectual reasoning, rationality, and objectivity) with inner knowing (deep wisdom, sense of wonder, introspection, and emotion). The books stress the development of the whole person and that educators should attend to all facets of our humanity—intellectual, social, emotional, and spiritual. In these books is the most cutting-edge information about contemplative pedagogy and its relationship to teacher education, including its uses, its challenges, and its promise. Epistemologically, these books move away from overprivileging René Descartes's "I think therefore I am," and toward modeling Audre Lorde's "I feel, therefore I can be free" (1984, p. 100). The authors get it right. Quite simply, education is not just about the mind; it is also about our emotions and about our social and spiritual development.

This collection of books plays an integral part in moving education to a new consciousness, one that challenges, if not shatters, hegemonic assumptions about teaching and learning, including the privileging of positivist assumptions about detachment and objectivity, Eurocentrism as the only credible way of knowing, the separation of teacher and student, and the separation of reason from emotion. What is being offered in these books is a politic of affinity and connectedness, and the ontological view that humanity at its core seeks relationships and a sense of belonging. Thinking and feeling share equal status and become, as Lorde expresses, "a choice of ways and explorations" (1984, p. 101) to seek knowledge and to form truths.

Book 1, *Cultivating a Culture of Learning: Contemplative Practices, Pedagogy, and Research in Education*, is targeted at educators who seek to learn from contemplative tools and pedagogic practices that will lead them to take the preparation of new educators to a higher level. This first book delivers careful discussion and nuanced understandings of terms and strategies. What is promising is that these approaches can work well across school settings—urban and rural, high- and low-income communities, and culturally diverse settings. Each chapter offers a portrait of practice written by authors who share firsthand experiences and who draw from original and existing research to engage a specific approach to teaching in diverse settings. Compositely, the chapters offer a newly constructed imaginary about teaching and learning. This pedagogic imaginary focuses on the following:

- an emphasis on wholeness and the relationship between inner and outer knowing
- the cultivation of what I call "una persona educada" (Rendón, 2011), a sage individual held in high regard who possesses knowledge and wisdom with a good measure of social and personal responsibility who also possesses the habits of the mind and heart
- a wide range of examples of contemplative tools and instructional strategies that generate deeper insights, for example, mindfulness and physical touchstones such as rocks, poetic verse, contemplative reading, cultivating compassion, mindful noticing, shared writing, digital storytelling, deep listening, authentic dialogue, global perspectives, private journaling, volunteerism, introspection, and contemplative online learning, among others
- competencies that can be cultivated in conjunction with a holistic approach to education including community orientation, compassion, empathy, open-mindedness, nonjudgment, and personal introspection, among others
- methods to reduce stress and to practice self-care for teacher candidates including mindfulness training, collegial support, and personal journaling

These three books should be required reading, especially for the new generation of students seeking to enter the teaching profession and who believe that values and ethical practices such as community, personal and social responsibility, integrity, truth telling, and self-reflection must share an equal space with cognitive development in a school classroom. Of significant import is that these books represent a marvelous pedagogic gift from courageous educators who have dared to take risks, have followed their intuition about what an authentic classroom should be, and have stayed true to the original impulse that drove them into the teaching profession.

I imagine that if you have picked up any one of these three books, something inside of you is seeking something different, something authentic, and something that speaks to the whole of your being. Look no more.

In your hands are exemplars of authentic teacher training, holistic student development, and the cultivation of classrooms guided by rigorous intellectual pursuits and the foundation for building an educational system that aspires to democratic ideals, humanitarianism, culturally responsive practices, and the common good. In your hands is the foundation for the evolution of a new story of what it means to prepare educators to facilitate student learning in a world that is desperately calling for ethical leaders who can (with intelligence, insight, and wisdom) deal with the contradictions, uncertainties, messiness, and complications of our lives.

I applaud this inspiring, groundbreaking work and encourage you to become an integral part of shaping the new story of education based on wholeness and guided by the ultimate expression of our values—love.

REFERENCES

Lorde, A. (1984). *Sister outsider: Essays and speeches*. Berkeley, CA: Crossing Press.
Hawkins, D. (2007). *The informed vision: Essays on learning and human nature*. New York: Algora.
Rendón, L. I. (2009). *Sentipensante pedagogy: Educating for wholeness, social justice and liberation*. Sterling, VA: Stylus.
Rendón, L. I. (2011). Cultivating una persona educada. A sentipensante (sending/thinking) vision of education. *Journal of College and Character, 12*(2), 1–9.

Acknowledgments

This book has been inspired and nurtured by many educators, artists, scholars, and contemplatives. Our heartfelt gratitude to those educators, past and present, who have been instrumental in opening the contemplative path and to the students whose search for meaning and purpose provided inspiration for and feedback during the journey.

We are grateful to all of those with whom we have had the pleasure to work with during the development and publication of this series of books. Without the vision and dedication of the volume one authors—Maureen Hall, Libby Falk Jones, Aminda J. O'Hare, Mary-Ann Mitchell-Pellett, Kristin N. Rainville, Katie Egan Cunningham, Jeremy Forest Price, Tami Augustine, Heather Bandeen, Elizabeth G. Holtzman, and Carolyn H. Obel-Omia—this series would not be possible. Each unique voice and perspective offers a richly complex tapestry of ways to integrate contemplative practice, pedagogy, and research into the field of teacher education. We extend a special thanks to Tom Koerner, Carlie Wall, and Emily Tuttle at Rowman & Littlefield for their support during this process. We are also especially grateful to Laura I. Rendón, professor emerita at the University of Texas-San Antonio, and author of *Sentipensante (Sensing/Thinking) Pedagogy: Educating for Wholeness, Social Justice, and Liberation* for writing the profound, inspired forewords for each of the three volumes in this series.

We feel especially humbled by the collaboration, support, friendship, and collegiality that has developed over the years as we, the editors, worked together to develop, refine, and publish this book series. We are honored to curate such a meaningful, inspired, and inspiring series of books for future generations of teacher educators, educators, and students.

Introduction

In recent years, contemplative pedagogy in teacher education has moved from being a niche pedagogical practice to being an emergent and relevant approach to teaching and learning in higher education classrooms. Contemplative pedagogy cultivates self-awareness and intrapersonal and interpersonal skills, and deepens learning through practices such as breath awareness, meditation, silence, Lectio Divina, and the arts. As with all emergent curriculum, relevant and timely discourse is needed to illuminate the multiple ways in which contemplative pedagogy strengthens teaching and learning in classrooms while simultaneously supporting teacher development.

Typically, teacher education dedicates significant time to build capacities learned from external authorities with an overemphasis on tips, tricks, and techniques of the profession. Rubrics, assessments, instructional strategies, curriculum mapping, and classroom management all privilege rational and empirical knowing across disciplines. Yet, if educators are prepared to rely solely on external authorities as a gauge for pedagogical decisions, then they fail to develop their full capacities, limiting their effectiveness.

Teaching and learning at its best is one of the most elemental of human exchanges and requires that we take responsibility for what, how, and why we teach, and who we are as teachers. David Hawkins (2007) suggests that meaningful learning experiences rely on three interdependent facets: *it*, the content of teaching; *thou*, who is being taught; and *I*, who is teaching. Opening the door to contemplation in teacher education facilitates teacher reflection that deepens content knowledge, relationships with students, and self-awareness of the I, as teacher.

Teaching demands we engage all dimensions of human awareness and action. As critical practitioners of the human experience, educators navigate several worlds: the inner realm of their personal life and the outer worlds of their classroom, students, and school. As Parker Palmer (1997) observes, "External tools of power have occasional utility in teaching, but they are no substitute for the authority that comes from the teacher's inner life. The clue is in the word itself, which has 'author' at its core" (p. 19). Educators become the authors of their lives and access the inner life through first-person contemplative experience, second-person dialogue and reflection in community, and third-person narratives of inspiration and guidance, through the integration of contemplative theory, research, and practice in teacher education.

The overwhelmingly positive response to our call for chapter submissions demonstrated an interest in the ways in which contemplative theory, research, and practices are being integrated into teacher education globally. We have organized this scholarship within the field of contemplative teacher education into three books that address the following themes: *Cultivating a Culture of Learning, Impacting Teaching and Learning*, and *The Teaching Self*. Together these books offer varying insights into the multiple ways that contemplative theory, practices, and research appear in teacher education. In each book, critical, global perspectives address the challenges of implementation along with the benefits of contemplative practices and pedagogy.

The first book focuses on the *it*, the integration of contemplative practices in teacher education courses and programs, which is often the most salient and pragmatic approach for teacher educators. The second book addresses the *thou*, current research on the impacts of contemplative practices and pedagogy in teacher education. The third book returns our attention to the teaching self, the *who*. It is our hope that these three volumes will contribute to the ongoing dialogue about contemplative pedagogy in teacher education.

The first book in this series, *Cultivating a Culture of Learning: Contemplative Practices, Pedagogy, and Research in Education*, illustrates portraits of practice from a variety of teacher education programs, bringing together a rich collection of voices from diverse settings. All of the authors in this book share their firsthand experience of opening to practice as teacher educators and employing contemplative practices in their work with educators. Several chapters offer innovative models, pedagogy, and courses utilizing contemplative practices. Authors explore challenges faced institutionally, with students, and personally. The following paragraphs offer highlights of each of the eight chapters in this book.

Chapter 1, "Internal Ways of Knowing: A Case for Contemplative Practices in Preservice Teacher Education," by Maureen Hall, Libby Falk Jones, and Aminda J. O'Hare, examines the rationale for and effects of introducing an eight-week mindfulness attention module into the first course of a teacher licensure program. Although our current system of education has not led to emotional and psychological success for all, evidence suggests that mindfulness training for preservice teachers may be one way to educate the "whole" person and prepare new teachers to address their future students on both emotional and cognitive levels. Participants in this study demonstrated self-reported personal growth, gains in psychological and physical health, and improved relationships with others.

Chapter 2, "Rock, Rock! Who's There?" by Mary-Ann Mitchell-Pellett, explores how river rocks were used as unique contemplative tools in a first-year teacher preparation course, which took place at an urban university in Alberta, Canada. These river companions supported students as they explored their emerging teacher identities by helping them to focus mindfully and become aware of the intersection among self, role, and values that were constantly being composed and recomposed as they learned to be teachers. The rocks were used symbolically and pedagogically to provide an opportunity for preservice teachers to connect to their inner and outer worlds, the aim being to enhance their abilities to fully engage with diverse learners and be attentive to the impact of their future students' inner and outer lives.

Chapter 3, "Reframing How We Think About Learning: A Four-Source Model," by Kristin N. Rainville and Katie Egan Cunningham, describes specific ways in which the authors integrate contemplative practices into undergraduate and graduate education courses designed for preservice teacher candidates. The chapter is structured using a Sanskrit shloka, or poetic verse, that describes learning as four sources for how we learn and grow. The four sources include learning from one's teacher, oneself, one's peers, and with time.

Chapter 4, "Using Contemplative Pedagogies to Explore Diversity within and beyond One's Experience in Preservice Teacher Education," by Jeremy Forest Price, charts the journey of undergraduate preservice teachers learning to recognize the uniqueness and diversity in themselves and others by developing contemplative and mindful inquiry practices. Most students in the course grew up in a predominantly rural Appalachian state where the prevailing narrative from inside and out was that the population was homogeneous and monolithic in terms of characteristics and outlook, despite evidence to the contrary. Contemplative pedagogy was a central feature of this course to support preservice teachers in recognizing their inner lives and the stories, narratives, and prejudices that may be conveyed about them as well as those they may convey about others.

Chapter 5, "Deep Listening, Authentic Dialogue: Supporting the Work of Critical Global Education," by Tami Augustine, examines the importance of integrating contemplative practices for preservice teachers to develop skills related to listening and dialogue. Deep listening and authentic dialogue practice help preservice teachers develop open-mindedness and value a shared sense of purpose in an interconnected global community. After an introduction of the intersections of contemplative practice and critical global education, the chapter provides classroom practices that supported the work of global education, with a focus on openness to new information, development of perspective consciousness, and understanding of multiple perspectives.

Chapter 6, "Toward Persistence: Contemplative Practices in Community College Teacher Education Programs," by Heather Bandeen, delves into the unique challenges of community college campuses and outlines a series of concrete strategies, including volunteering, developing spatial awareness, and ongoing reflection, all designed to bolster student persistence. These practices can yield unique benefits for community college students while also offering universal pedagogical models that support all preservice teacher candidates.

Chapter 7, "Mindfulness and Student Teaching: Practice Makes Perfect (Just as You Are!)," by Elizabeth G. Holtzman and Carolyn H. Obel-Omia, focuses on the essential need for self-care, given the high level of demands and performance pressure during preservice teacher education. Preservice teachers experience many of the same challenges as beginning teachers in our current education culture of increasing accountability. One way to support preservice teachers in managing this stress is through mindfulness training to support their own wellness, something often overlooked due to focusing on performance. This chapter describes a cross-disciplinary collaboration supporting the introduction of mindfulness practice in an elementary education preservice teacher seminar.

Chapter 8, "Across Time and Space: Designing Online Contemplative Learning," by Kathryn Byrnes, discusses the ways in which contemplative pedagogy is not limited to face-to-face, synchronous learning. Designing contemplative, online learning environments for preservice and in-service educators offers several challenges that require skillful management of technology, people, time, and resources. Using a case from a hybrid course titled Mindful Education, six paradoxical tensions described by Palmer (1998) are applied to an online contemplative course for educators, and the impact they have on contemplative course design and pedagogy is analyzed.

Opening to contemplative practice in teacher education demands courageous commitment and willingness to step into the unknown and model authentic engagement through compassionate, experiential personal practice. The authors in this book advocate and express the importance of creating spaces where the inner life and qualities such as intuition, creativity, silence, and heart-centered learning are valued and work in partnership with cognitive and rational ways of knowing and being in the world. The insights and challenges shared in these portraits of practice are intended to stimulate conversation and engender future pedagogy and research in the field of contemplative teacher education.

REFERENCES

Hawkins, D. (2007). *The informed vision: Essays on learning and human nature*. New York: Algora.

Palmer, P. J. (1997). The heart of a teacher: Identity and integrity in teaching. *Change Magazine, 29*(6), 14–21.

Palmer, P. J. (1998). *The courage to teach: Exploring the inner landscape of a teacher's life*. San Francisco: Jossey-Bass.

Chapter One

Internal Ways of Knowing

A Case for Contemplative Practices in
Preservice Teacher Education

Maureen Hall, University of Massachusetts
Dartmouth, Dartmouth, Massachusetts;
Libby Falk Jones, Berea College, Berea, Kentucky;
Aminda J. O'Hare, University of Massachusetts
Dartmouth, Dartmouth, Massachusetts

Everyone has been made for some particular work, and the desire for that work has been put in every heart.—Rumi

Today's K–12 teachers must meet extensive demands. Teachers in secular settings are expected to teach an academic curriculum, train students to be ethical and upstanding citizens, and cultivate students' emotional and psychological skills. The many demands on educators and learners today require a multitude of skills to produce critical thinkers and problem solvers. Despite these increasing demands, a curriculum that incorporates the development of resiliency, coping, and well-being in preservice educators has not been widely adopted.

In spite of extensive efforts by teachers at all levels, our current system of education has not led to emotional and psychological success for all. Success in education must involve education of the "whole" person, reaching students on both emotional and cognitive levels and allowing for full development of human potential. Without activating both cognitive and affective dimensions of human consciousness, learning does not endure (Owen-Smith, 2004; Waxler & Hall, 2011).

Holistic educator Jack Miller draws on the words of Harry Lewis, former dean of Harvard College, as he warns of the danger that our schools will become "soulless" places (Miller, 2014, p. 69). Lewis argues that a student is viewed as a "brain on a stick" (Lewis, 2006, p. 100), and this disturbing image seems to capture what is happening today in schools. These academic climates that reduce intrinsic motivation of teachers and students are associated with increased teacher burnout (Pietarinen, Pyhalto, Soini, & Salmela-Aro, 2013), so they also impact occupational success.

Dehumanizing education ultimately damages society as a whole. In the foreword to *Contemplative Practices in Higher Education*, Parker Palmer notes that for many of today's leaders, "expert knowledge—and the power that comes with it—has not been joined to a professional ethic, a sense of communal responsibility, or even simple compassion" (Barbezat & Bush, 2014, p. vii).

Palmer and other educators argue for a more integrative approach to education, for learning that is grounded within the individual (Glazer, 1999, p. 1) and the relationships among individuals (Pianta, Hamre, & Allen, 2012). These scholars investigate ways that "education can serve as the core of a lifelong journey toward wholeness, rather than merely an accumulation of facts, figures, or skills" (Glazer, 1999, p. 3).

One promising approach is through integrating mindfulness in the form of contemplative practices. Though all students can benefit from contemplative practices that encourage whole learning, such education is especially important in the preservice teacher classroom, as these students are future teachers and ultimately have some power to transform education itself.

Some benefits of contemplative practice for preservice teachers include reflecting on their own learning processes in the classroom as students as well as metacognitively imagining their effectiveness as pedagogical guides for their own students' learning and transformation. A recent meta-analysis on the impact of contemplative practices in education found increases in cognitive ability and resiliency and decreases in stress (Zenner, Hermleben-Kurz, & Walach, 2014). Instilling these benefits in the next generation of teachers could in turn benefit students through improved engagement by and relationships with their teachers.

In this chapter, various contemplative practices in higher education are explored. Then an introductory teacher education course taught at a public university in the Northeast in spring 2015 in which mindfulness attention practices were integrated is described. This description draws on students' responses to illustrate the challenges and rewards of pursuing contemplative pedagogies in the preservice teacher classroom.

CONTEMPLATIVE PRACTICES: HISTORICAL AND
PHILOSOPHICAL BACKGROUND

Contemplative practices in education in the United States have a long history. For example, Patricia Morgan (2014) recounts that contemplative orientation in U.S. education was initiated when Buddhism was introduced to schools through the children of the Chinese immigration in 1840. The second stage came in the 1960s and 1970s with the establishment of three educational institutions: the California Institute for Integral Studies, Naropa University in Colorado, and the Maharishi University of Management in Iowa. Palmer explains why these institutions are different from many other higher education institutions: they challenge the objectivist model of knowing, teaching, and learning that "insists on a wall of separation between the knower and the known" (Barbezat & Bush, 2014, p. vii).

In 1995, Morgan argues, the third stage or reemergence of contemplative education began. Morgan (2014) identifies the beginning of this stage with the founding of the Center for Contemplative Mind in Society (p. 1). Most certainly, there is a much longer history of contemplative practices in education in other parts of the world. In fact, the original roots of much of what we call "present moment learning" originated in ancient India (e.g., Mookerji, 2003), where the central focus was on "developing focused awareness in individuals, and ethical service for society" (Waxler & Hall, 2011, p. 111).

Yet roadblocks to contemplative approaches to education have also emerged. In the early seventeenth century, contemplative practices were considered suspect by some in Europe. For example, René Descartes seemingly disconnected the mind from the body. Gary Young and Monica Whitty (2010) argue that when Descartes announced, "I think, therefore I am," the human being was "transformed, reduced even, to a disembodied mind" (p. 209).

The "Cartesian moment" is described as a shifting in "the history of Western thought where contemplative practices, as a part of care of the self in the context of community and cosmos were divorced from academic pursuits" (Gunnlaugson, Sarath, Scott, & Bai, 2014, p. 1). Thus the twenty-first-century educational controversy of neglecting mind-body-spirit connections has persisted for several centuries.

Recent scholarship explores the repercussions of this disruption and suggests some means to regain wholeness. Palmer (1993) argues that rather than investigating connections between the self and the world, conventional education strives "to get [the self] out of the way" (p. 35). Palmer notes that widespread suffering has flowed from this fundamental disconnection and suggests pursuing spiritually grounded pedagogies through which "knowing becomes a reunion of separated beings" (p. 32).

Palmer's critique and suggested response are echoed by Jeffrey Wilhelm and Bruce Novak (2011). These authors want to replace what they term our "systematically-deadening regime" with a "thoroughly thought-through life-enhancing agenda" (p. 9). That agenda encourages learners to become trans-active and responsive to their learning and to the world, not passive consumers of knowledge. Psychologist Ellen Langer (2016) also focuses on learners, arguing that learners must become more mindful. Langer argues that teachers can help students cultivate mindful learning habits, including becoming open to alternatives and aware of distinctions (pp. 19, 23).

Other researchers' findings suggest that mindfulness practices can help students to regulate their emotions, increase their attentional capacities, and create positive habits of mind (e.g., Davidson et al., 2012). Contemplative practices serve to integrate mind and body toward awareness of the present moment and help cultivate wisdom, thus creating openness to new information (O'Reilley, 1998).

The spread of knowledge about the benefits of contemplative practices has led to implementation in a variety of locales. In *Contemplative Learning and Inquiry across Disciplines*, Olen Gunnlaugson and colleagues (2014) cite recent work with contemplative approaches at several institutions. They view this explosion of contemplative approaches to studies as a "poignant sign that the current life-world situation of our time is one that needs to regain a measure of dynamic balance, wisdom, and intelligence" (p. 1). For example, programs such as MindUP (http://thehawnfoundation.org/mindup), designed to train students and teachers how to self-regulate behavior and engage in concentration, are being integrated into K–12 classrooms.

In addition, professional organizations, such as the Center for Contemplative Mind in Society and its initiative, the Association for Contemplative Mind in Higher Education, are facilitating the development of contemplative studies initiatives across educational institutions (see www .contemplativemind.org). The University of Miami's Mindfulness Research and Practice Initiative and the University of Virginia's Contemplative Science Center are teaching and studying contemplative practices not only in education but also in the professional world. This broader vision of education and human development is needed in order to create educated individuals who contribute to the betterment of society.

BENEFITS OF MINDFULNESS PRACTICES

Traditionally, contemplative practices, particularly mindfulness, have been used by clinical psychologists as an effective intervention for treating a range of psychological disorders, including anxiety and depression (Hofmann, Sawyer, Witt, & Oh, 2010). The improvement in symptoms associated with mindfulness has been attributed to the fact that this technique utilizes cognitive strategies that strengthen executive functions, such as sustaining attention, flexibly switching the focus of attention, and inhibiting elaborative processing (Bishop et al., 2004). Most support for these cognitive improvements has come from neuroimaging research.

These studies have shown increases in both gray and white matter in areas of the brain involved with cognitive control, or the ability to stay goal focused and inhibit distracting information, as well as areas involved in emotional regulation (e.g., Boccia, Piccardi, & Guariglia, 2015). Because these areas of the brain seem strengthened by mindfulness meditation practice, it can be inferred that the cognitive abilities with which they have been associated also improve.

Research using functional measures of brain activity has supported this inference by finding reduced activation in areas of the brain associated with mind wandering (Brewer et al., 2011) and emotional reactivity (Desbordes et al., 2012) in individuals with mindfulness meditation experience. Additionally, increased activation or more efficient activation in areas of the brain associated with cognitive control has been found in experienced meditators and individuals undergoing eight- to sixteen-week training sessions, respectively (Ives-Deliperi, Solms, & Meintjes, 2011; Moore, Gruber, Derose, & Malinowski, 2012).

This wealth of psychological and neuroscientific support for the impact of contemplative practices on cognitive and emotional regulation strategies is driving the push for increased integration of such practices into our educational environments. Theoretically, implementing contemplative practices into preservice teacher education would increase the ability of future teachers to stay focused and present in the classroom, be less reactive to classroom disruptions, experience reduced rates of burnout, and foster better connections with their students.

INTEGRATING MINDFULNESS PRACTICES INTO A CORE COURSE FOR PRESERVICE TEACHERS: CHALLENGES AND BENEFITS

An eight-week mindfulness attention module was introduced into the course Fundamentals of Teaching and Learning at the University of Massachusetts Dartmouth, in spring 2015. There were eighteen students in the course, primarily juniors and seniors planning to pursue the master of arts in teaching (MAT) and teacher licensure. This first course in the sequence aimed to introduce these potential teachers to the real world of teaching through exploring theories of human development and learning; the history, philosophy, sociology, and politics of American education today; current educational issues, trends, and reform movements; and the challenges and rewards of teaching.

Students also completed fifteen field study practicum hours in a K–12 classroom experience. Integrating mindfulness practices was designed to cultivate the preservice teachers' social-emotional capacities. All students gave written, informed consent to have their data collected from this project reported in an anonymous format.

Mindfulness training in Fundamentals of Teaching and Learning occurred over eight weeks, beginning in the fourth week of the course. The mindfulness sessions were based on the traditional Mindfulness-Based Stress Reduction trainings developed by Jon Kabat-Zinn (e.g., 1982). Each week, the students learned about a new way to practice mindfulness and discussed new concepts related to the practice of mindfulness during the class session.

Mindfulness topics and practices included the following:

- breath-focused seated meditation, principles of letting go of thoughts and acceptance of the present (weeks one and two);
- walking meditation, mindfulness of thoughts (week three);
- attending to positive emotion, mindfulness and emotions (week four);
- mindful eating, attending to negative emotions, beginner's mind (approaching the present without expectation) (week five);
- body scans (systematically attending to sensations from the body), non-striving (having no expectations of outcome) (week six);
- loving-kindness meditation (attending to positive thoughts toward the self), patience (week seven); and
- loving-kindness meditation toward others, nonjudgment (not evaluating one's experiences) (week eight).

Students were asked to practice the techniques outside class during that week and to reflect on their experiences in their online mindfulness reflection journals. They were asked to comment on what they learned about the self and others through the exercises as well as to note how they experienced the actual mindful practices. Students reported both challenges and rewards from the mindfulness practices.

Challenges included distractions, feeling silly, impatience, and negative emotions. "My patience for sitting is not that great," one wrote, adding, "I feel like my mind is wandering." Another wrote of the challenge of practicing loving-kindness toward a disliked person: "Saying the words didn't feel right. . . . All I could think of was the horrible things the person did." Most students (fourteen of eighteen) reported progress in coping with these challenges and in developing elements of social-emotional competence.

The Collaborative for Academic, Social, and Emotional Learning (CASEL) lists five social and emotional competencies: self-awareness, self-management, social awareness, relationship skills, and responsible decision-making (as cited in Dorman, 2015). Elizabeth Dorman (2015) connects social-emotional learning to another theoretical framework as set forth by Laura Weaver and Mark Wilding's engaged teaching approach (2013). Dorman (2015) cites research showing that "building teachers' social-emotional competence, including via mindfulness training, can improve teachers' overall effectiveness and help equip them with the tools needed to respond to the unique stressors of the teaching profession" (p. 4).

Students' self-reflections provided insight into their experience with social-emotional competence. Twelve of the eighteen students noted gains in self-awareness and self-management. Some observations included the following: "Before doing schoolwork for several hours, I have found that meditating helps me to clear my mind and get into a working mindset." Attention to breathing also led to increased self-awareness and self-management. One student wrote of becoming "increasingly aware of my lung capacity. . . . Thoughts came in but I was able to gently dismiss and file them." Another found that sitting practice went well: "After a long day, I followed a guide where you had to focus on your breathing, and I was able to do that well without many distractions."

Walking meditation was particularly useful in developing these self-awareness and self-management abilities. One student wrote, "I am able to focus on my slow-motion walking that keeps me in the present. Once I am distracted . . . I feel myself stumble or lose balance a little, which brings me back." Another student who engaged in regular mindful walking (twenty to thirty minutes daily) wrote, "I really started to enjoy it and . . . latch onto my surroundings as an anchor in the present moment."

Self-management gains included student-reported perceived health benefits, particularly from practicing an eating meditation. "One thing I've really noticed is how much I've slowed down my eating," one student wrote, adding, "I also noticed I've lost ten pounds since we went over eating meditation." Another wrote, "I never realized how much I don't pay attention to anything I eat." Other students responded positively to body scans. "Scans at night are a blessing; [it] relaxes my whole body and allows me to get a good night's rest."

In addition to strengthening these self-directed competencies, twelve of the eighteen students noted increased development of the three competencies directed toward others: social awareness, relationship skills, and responsible decision making. "I have been very mindfully refocusing myself to the present moment very regularly in many aspects of my life," wrote one student, "especially those times that I have spent with my kids, reading, snuggling, hugging, listening to them and watching their emotions and responses rather than moving through the motions of the day without noticing these things."

Focusing on the breath and "spot on the floor" also helped the student who reported difficulties with practicing loving-kindness toward another: "I felt myself actually feeling sympathetic for the person this session and actually thinking it wasn't their fault they annoyed me at times." Most students (fourteen of eighteen) indicated that they felt more comfortable with mindfulness practices toward the end of the training. "I notice myself using fragments of all the mindfulness training throughout my entire day," one wrote.

CONCLUSION

Our current attempts with integrating mindfulness meditation practices into preservice teacher education suggest that these practices can help students cope with the stresses of their professional and personal lives. Students' reflections demonstrated self-reported personal growth, gains in psychological and physical health, and improved relationships with others. Theoretically, if these practices were continued and supported in K–12 schools, these teachers would be more engaged in their teaching, more resilient to workplace and life stressors, better able to listen to and connect with their students, and better colleagues and members of the larger school community.

As Palmer (1998) notes, teachers must be in community with themselves before being able to create community among others. To be in community with oneself requires managing one's emotions. A former teacher, Patricia Jennings (2015), points out that teachers are expected to have developed these abilities, despite the fact that most teachers "received little if any explicit preservice or in-service training aimed at [their] own personal development" (p. 38). Our mindfulness intervention suggests that mindfulness practices can help preservice teachers learn to manage their emotions.

It requires time to transform education and build community; individuals need time to get to know one another and feel affiliated, to create trust, and to discover shared goals. While progress was seen in our eight-week intervention, continuing these practices over time is needed to make long-term changes in the five social-emotional capacities. To make this model sustainable, the education community at large needs to be committed to creating the time and space for contemplative work and to prioritize this work.

We call for an adjustment in teacher education and K–12 culture, where the social and emotional abilities of teachers are valued as highly as their ability to teach classroom content. When mindfulness practices are implemented within the preservice teacher classroom, teachers and learners can "co-create a community for learning where everyone feels valued" (Hall, 2005, p. 8). Mindfulness practices can provide an important step toward creating classrooms where learners—and teachers—can function as dynamic human beings with innate and unlimited potential.

ESSENTIAL IDEAS TO CONSIDER

- Current climates in education are leading to increased teacher burnout, feelings of fragmentation, and inability to be attentive to students' needs.
- The skill of mindfulness provides an avenue for teachers to cope with stress and feelings of fragmentation, leading to better connections with their profession and their students.
- In one graduate education course, eight weeks of mindfulness led to reported increases in social-emotional development.
- Instilling these skills in preservice teachers can lead to a shift in educational climates toward valuing intra- and interpersonal ability in concert with academic ability.
- Mindfulness training holds possibilities for improving teacher engagement and thus, ultimately, student engagement.

REFERENCES

Barbezat, D. P., & Bush, M. (2014). *Contemplative practices in higher education: Powerful methods to transform teaching and learning.* San Francisco: Jossey-Bass.

Bishop, S. R., Lau, M., Shapiro, S., Carlson, L., Anderson, N. D., Carmody, J., . . . Devins, G. (2004). Mindfulness: A proposed operational definition. *Clinical Psychology: Science and Practice, 11*(3), 230–241.

Boccia, M., Piccardi, L., & Guariglia, P. (2015). The meditative mind: A comprehensive meta-analysis of MRI studies. *BioMed Research International,* 1–11.

Brewer, J. A., Worhunsky, P. D., Gray, J. R., Tang, Y., Weber, J., & Kober, H. (2011). Mediation experience is associated with differences in default mode network activity and connectivity. *PNAS, 108*(50), 20254–20259.

Davidson, R., Dunne, J., Eccles, J. S., Engle, A., Greenberg, M., Jennings, P., . . . Vago, D. (2012). Contemplative practices and mental training: Prospects for American education. *Child Development Perspectives, 6*(2), 146–153.

Desbordes, G., Negi, L. T., Pace, T. W. W., Wallace, B. A., Raison, C. L., & Schwartz, E. L. (2012). Effects of mindful-attention and compassion meditation training on amygdala response to emotional stimuli in an ordinary, non-meditative state. *Frontiers in Human Neuroscience, 6*(292), 1–15.

Dorman, E. (2015). Building teachers' social-emotional competence through mindful practices. *Curriculum and Teaching Dialogue, 17*(1–2), 103–119.

Glazer, S. (Ed.). (1999). *The heart of learning.* New York: TarcherPerigee.

Gunnlaugson, O., Sarath, E. W., Scott, C., & Bai, H. (Eds.). (2014). *Contemplative learning and inquiry across disciplines.* New York: SUNY Press.

Hall, M. P. (2005). Bridging the heart and mind: Community as a device for linking cognitive and affective learning. *Journal of Cognitive Affective Learning, 1,* 8–12.

Hofmann, S. G., Sawyer, A. T., Witt, A. A., & Oh, D. (2010). The effect of mindfulness-based therapy on anxiety and depression: A meta-analytic review. *Journal of Consulting Clinical Psychology, 78*(2), 169–183.

Ives-Deliperi, V. L., Solms, M., & Meintjes, E. M. (2011). The neural substrates of mindfulness: An fMRI investigation. *Social Neuroscience, 6*(3), 231–242.

Jennings, P. A. (2015). Mindfulness for teachers: Simple skills for peace and productivity in the classroom. New York: Norton.

Kabat-Zinn, J. (1982). An outpatient program in behavioral medicine for chronic pain patients based on the practice of mindfulness meditation: Theoretical considerations and preliminary results. *General Hospital Psychiatry, 4*(1), 33–47.

Langer, E. J. (2016). *The power of mindful learning*. Boston: Da Capo.

Lewis, H. (2006). *Excellence without a soul? Does liberal education have a future?* New York: Public Affairs.

Miller, J. P. (2014). Contemplation: The soul's way of knowing. In O. Gunnlaugson, E. W. Sarath, C. Scott, & H. Bai (Eds.), *Contemplative learning and inquiry across disciplines* (pp. 69–81). New York: SUNY Press.

Mookerji, R. K. (2003). *Ancient Indian education: Brahmanical and Buddhist*. New Delhi, India: Motilal Barnarsi Dass. (Original work published 1947)

Moore, A., Gruber, T., Derose, J., & Malinowski, P. (2012). Regular, brief mindfulness meditation practice improves electrophysiological markers of attentional control. *Frontiers in Human Neuroscience, 6*(18), 1–15.

Morgan, P. F. (2014). A brief history of the current reemergence of contemplative education. *Journal of Transformative Education, 13*(1), 1–22.

O'Reilley, M. R. (1998). *Radical presence: Teaching as contemplative practice*. Portsmouth, NH: Heinemann.

Owen-Smith, P. (2004). What is cognitive-affective learning? *Journal of Cognitive Affective Learning, 1*(1). Retrieved June 10, 2016, from http://www.jcal.emory.edu.

Palmer, P. J. (1993). *To know as we are known: Education as a spiritual journey* (2nd ed.). San Francisco: HarperCollins.

Palmer, P. J. (1998). *The courage to teach: Exploring the inner landscape of a teacher's life*. San Francisco: Jossey-Bass.

Pianta, R. C., Hamre, B. K., & Allen, J. P. (2012). Teacher-student relationships and engagement: Conceptualizing, measuring, and improving the capacity of classroom interactions. In S. L. Christenson, A. L. Reschly, & C. Wylie (Eds.), *Handbook of research on student engagement* (pp. 365–386). New York: Springer-Verlag.

Pietarinen, J., Pyhalto, K., Soini, T., & Salmela-Aro, K. (2013). Reducing teacher burnout: A socio-contextual approach. *Teaching and Teacher Education, 35*, 62–72.

Waxler, R. P., & Hall, M. P. (2011). *Transforming literacy: Changing lives through reading and writing*. Bingley, UK: Emerald Group.

Weaver, L. & Wilding, M. (2013). *The 5 dimensions of engaged teaching: A practical guide for educators*. Bloomington, IN: Solution Tree Press.

Wilhelm, J., & Novak, B. (2011). *Teaching literacy for love and wisdom: Being the book and being the change*. New York: Teachers College Press.

Young, G., & Whitty, M. (2010). In search of the Cartesian self: An examination of disembodiment within 21st-century communication. *Theory and Psychology, 20*(2), 209–229.

Zenner, C., Hermleben-Kurz, S., & Walach, H. (2014). Mindfulness-based interventions in schools: A systematic review and meta-analysis. *Frontiers in Psychology, 5*(603), 1–20.

Chapter Two

Rock, Rock! Who's There?

Mary-Ann Mitchell-Pellett, University of Calgary, Calgary, Alberta

If it weren't for the rocks in its bed, the stream would have no song.
—Carl Perkins (Lydon, 1968)

While observing a stream, it is amazing to watch the steady ability of pebbles and stones to combine harmoniously and naturally with the continuous flow of water they help sing to life. The rocks provide a sounding board, as water tumbles and flows over them, trickling, tinkling, bubbling, and swishing on its way. Akin to the unique sounds that rocks give to a streambed, could these same rocks make visible the voices, thoughts, and songs of beginning teachers as they began a formational process that invited inquiry and openness to their evolving authentic teacher selves?

Could rocks, yes rocks, be an effective tool for preservice teachers as they explored aspects of their stable yet changing values, selves, and roles, within a community of peers, forming a bedrock of contemplative professional practices, both literally and metaphorically? The answer to these questions is a resounding yes!

This chapter will explore how rocks were employed as a contemplative tool with first-year preservice teachers in a course titled Pragmatics of Teaching and Learning, which took place at an urban university in Alberta, Canada. The hope was that the rocks would serve as a contemplative tool for students to explore their teacher identities and guide their footing in the uncertain educational streambeds they were entering. How so?

The rocks symbolically and pedagogically could help students to mindfully become aware of their evolving identities and values as teachers. Additionally, the rocks could deepen insight into how the inner life of the teacher impacts the quality of his or her outer doing. Teachers need to be safe guides

11

for their students; as Rachael Kessler (2000) cautioned, what is not seen in oneself can "catch us from behind, grab us by the tail and swing us around" (p. 11), causing a loss of balance and perspective.

THE COURSE: THE PRAGMATICS OF TEACHING AND LEARNING

Pragmatics of Teaching and Learning is a required first-year course for all preservice teachers and is combined with students' first practicum teaching experience in the field. Halfway into the course, during the fall semester, students complete a two-week field practicum in a K–12 school, and then return to the pragmatics class for the remainder of the semester. Most of the instructors, including myself, for the pragmatics course were also the field instructors, and thus received the added benefit of witnessing theory in action for students during the practicum.

In my section, rock companions were incorporated throughout the entire semester as preservice teachers explored essential elements inherent in the aims of the course connected to developing teacher identity, exploring beliefs and perceptions of teaching, learning, and school culture, and becoming aware of the pragmatic realities of learning and teaching.

Although the course outline and assignments were predetermined by a course administrator, it was conceived that the essential questions and course content could provide an effective opening for students to explore the forma-tional layers of their teacher selves, including the intertwining paradox of self and role. Although preservice teachers were learning how to be in the role of the teacher, they were invited to contemplate that "I am also in the role of being me" (Noordhoff, 2012, p. 55).

Supporting preservice teachers as they make sense of themselves as teachers is preferable "before it makes sense for them to leave" the profes-sion when they are plagued with uncertainty of who they are and who they are becoming (Clandinin et al., 2012, p. 4).

Thus, a select bag of rocks and pebbles joined our class for the semester, and they were used contemplatively to further students' understanding of themselves and their roles as teachers by cultivating "a critical, first-person focus, sometimes with direct experience as the object, while at other times concentrating on complex ideas or situations" (Center for Contemplative Mind in Society, 2015, para. 1). The following sections will describe how the rocks were used as contemplative tools as preservice teachers developed their capacities for teaching and learning in formational and transformational ways, as well as the lessons learned from the interactions with the unassum-ing, yet empowering, rock companions.

WHO AM I? *SPARK* ROCKS

Throughout the pragmatics course, one aim was to have students develop their identities as newly emerging teachers and to become aware of how their beliefs and perceptions shape their view of students, schools, and teaching and learning. However, to do this well, students needed opportunities to learn how to be present to themselves and others. Hence, students were provided time to contemplate their unique identities and how this impacts the role of teacher. Through contemplative practice, students explored the connections between self and role, through potential openings and crevices related to identity, purpose, and empathy for self and others.

One entry point included Peter Benson's (2008) "sparks" (p. 2) concept whereby students were recognized as embodying something inside of the self that longed to be named and put into the world—a spark, a light that helped to make them come alive. Contemplating sparks was a natural way to initiate the process of self-exploration, as sparks have an inner origin and provide "a prime source of meaning, self-directed action, and purpose" (p. 19). This inquiry was contemplative as it facilitated "the natural human capacity for knowing through silence, looking inward, pondering deeply" (Hart, 2004, p. 29).

The activity was initiated by first having students choose some rocks and silently hold them, one by one, while contemplating things they loved to do in the world. Later, students journaled their insights and drew representations of their sparks upon the rocks. Some of the sparks that students identified included gifts or talents in areas related to sports, visual arts, dancing, writing, numbers, or technological skills. Others were related to qualities of being, such as being a good listener, being compassionate, or knowing when others needed help. While this activity gave students the opportunity to identify what brought them to life, they were also required to identify and describe at least five ways their sparks contributed to becoming the excellent teachers the world so very much needed.

The preservice teachers readily made connections between living one's passion or spark and the facilitation of highly engaged classrooms and students. For example, students compared their findings of the spark activity to a course reading that identified a reciprocal relationship between engaged classrooms and alignment with one's passion (Jacobsen, Lock, & Friesen, 2013).

Through identifying their own sparks, preservice teachers deepened their awareness about creating a live encounter for their students and themselves, when they integrated who they are and what they love with teaching and learning. Students shared how a spark became the primary reason they decided to become teachers and allow them to share their passion with others. This insight also revealed how teachers could be "Spark Champions" (Benson, 2008, p. 19) for their students' sparks and use them as a catalyst for joyful learning.

Additionally, students became aware that this inward approach to learning required a certain level of vulnerability not typically practiced in an outwardly focused Western culture. Contemplative work that connects the heart and head can look and feel messy (Palmer & Zajonc, 2010) and stir up feelings of vulnerability as it involves daring "to show up and let ourselves be seen" (Brown, 2012, p. 2). However, vulnerability also facilitates teaching with purpose and connection, as it is authenticity and realness that students look for in their teachers. Without vulnerability, identity formation and connection is challenging, and contemplative invitations were provided to develop further vulnerability and consequently better connection with the self and others.

However, there were a couple students who were resistant to the rock exercises. This resistance served as a reminder to offer choices for contemplative practice. Did some student require the shade of a tree instead of a rock?

Contemplative practices come in many forms, including "meditation, focused thought, time in nature, writing, contemplative arts, and contemplative movement" (Center for Contemplative Mind in Society, 2015, para. 3). Thus, providing alternative options for students to engage in contemplatively was established by making available writing, drawing, or other materials such as clay to interact with instead of rocks. Some students preferred to engage in drawing or writing, instead of rocks, to quiet the mind and aid exploration.

KALEIDOSCOPES OF IDENTITY

Armed with awareness acquired through previous contemplative practices in the class, the rock companions were engaged in another activity to cultivate cultural awareness. Some of the pragmatics course materials aimed to identify and develop positive school culture. However, before exploring the broader realms of this topic, students examined their personal cultural identities and how these might influence the spaces where school and classroom cultures are developed. Drawing on the work of Sandra Collins and Nancy Arthur (2010), we discussed cultural identity as a "kaleidoscope" (p. 70) of many intersecting multiple identities composed of personal, ideological, cultural, contextual, and universal elements.

To begin, students first spent time in silent contemplation, deeply listening to their thoughts and insights related to their cultural identities, and then they drew representative symbols related to their cultural selves onto the rocks. Students later shifted from deep listening of the self to contemplative dialogue with their peers. In groups of four, they were invited to be fully present to each other, practicing deep listening as each person shared—without interruption or questions. The rocks provided a symbolic representation of students' cultured identities, inviting vulnerability and shared awareness through metaphor.

Students responded extremely well to this exercise, and several mentioned that although they found the exercise challenging, they appreciated the invitation to uncover previously unknown aspects of self. A few students related that "no one has ever asked me to consider this before." Another student later wrote a poem generated from this exercise, which eloquently described his cultural identity, as well as his appreciation of the cultural identities of his peers. Several students expressed that they would use this activity with their own students, to cultivate knowledge and appreciation of cultural diversity, as well as facilitate qualities related to deep listening and empathy stimulated by the contemplative process.

As a follow-up to this activity, students were invited to work silently in groups to communally create a 3-D group rock/pebble installation that reflected the essential elements of a positive classroom culture. Most of the installations contained webs of interconnecting lines of pebbles that portrayed connections between students, teachers, the curriculum, and schools. Through communal contemplation, students collectively understood and expressed that their work as teachers and the building of a positive school and classroom was the result of centering not only on the self but also on the values inherent in positive learning cultures and others.

DIVERSITY AND VOICE: ROCKFISH

One of the major pragmatic realities with which preservice teachers need to contend is the complex diversity of their students and schools. An important aspect of developing an understanding of diversity includes creating opportunities for the voices of others to be cultivated and listened to, including students who are often marginalized people in our society and who are fearful of speaking their truth (O'Reilley, 1998). A fundamental role of teachers, who are well informed about diversity, is to welcome their students' voices and help "hear them into speech" (Morton, 1977, p. 205).

It was important to realize that preservice teachers are also students—many struggling with believing that what they had to say was worthy of being listened to. Thus, an opportunity was created for students to explore their diverse voices and to declare, "This is me!" Experiencing and honoring one's own wisdom, knowledge, and voice includes giving permission for these to be uncovered and then confidently making them known. If teachers are to act with any moral agency and justice for their students, then they must act with moral agency and justice for themselves as well, which starts by valuing their own voice and wisdom as human beings.

Utilizing the storybook *Only One You*, by Linda Krantz (2006), proved to be a worthwhile venture that allowed students to contemplate aspects of their diverse and unique voices that they may not have considered. All the characters in the storybook are uniquely and beautifully painted rocks that resembled fish, called rockfish, and the pages are filled with many wise phrases of encouragement related to being oneself, some of which included "You don't have to follow the crowd"; "Set aside some quiet time to relax and reflect each day"; and "Be you."

Students were invited to paint and decorate a rock in a manner that represented their own personal and human uniqueness, and later these rockfish selves were shared with their peers through one-to-one sharing. Afterward, we laid out all the unique rockfish in a circle, and students were invited to silently behold the beauty and the impressions that invited them to come closer. Everyone oohed and aahed in admiration of the beautiful array of diversity that came to life through the rocks. Students shared that they were grateful for the invitation to explore the diversity of their human and teacher selves, and to also share their thoughts about the unique types of teachers they wanted to become.

Further conversations stemming from this activity centered on how teachers could hold a space for their visions of personal and professional integrity within educational cultures that often demand compliance and devalued the freshness and wisdom that many young teachers offer. Maintaining authentic identity and integrity is essential to guarding the selfhood from where "all good teaching comes" (Palmer, 1998, p. 10). Students contemplated individually and in small groups, "How do I manifest who I am with integrity at this moment?" (Poutiatine & Conners, 2012, p. 67). Answers were varied, but many students agreed that having an effective awareness of one's identity as a human being and a teacher is an important first step.

By inviting students to explore and experience their own and others' diverse selves, the intention was that they would cultivate similar experiences for their students and feel sustained by the richness and diversity they were bringing to the profession of teaching. Too often, preservice teachers are identified through what they do not know or skills they do not have, which does not help to sustain their sense of agency and competency (Clandinin et al., 2012). Explorations with the rockfish gave preservice teachers permission to be and do teaching with authenticity and integrity, the bedrock of diversity.

PERSPECTIVE TAKING: ROCK PUPILS

Closely aligned with the practice of honoring diversity is the process of perspective taking. In preparation for Field Experience 1 in K–12 classrooms, students were introduced to the principles and practices of Universal Design for Learning (UDL), which is an educational approach used to accommodate diverse learners. In planning for diversity, students created a pseudo rock pupil and an accompanying learning profile that detailed their rock pupil's academic, social, and emotional needs.

Students decorated their rock pupils with googly eyes, faux hair, eyeglasses, crutches, hats, and other outward representations of their unique characteristics. Students were encouraged to create a rock pupil that was not a mini-me version of their own selves but instead in direct contrast to their own profile as a learner, to ensure the perspective-taking experience would be as authentic as possible.

With their rock pupils in tow, students set out for their field experience, with the instruction to answer their daily reflective questions using the perspectives of their teacher self and their rock pupil. For example, one of the daily questions required preservice teachers to journal about the effectiveness of an assessment strategy based on observations in their practicum placement. Thus, students responded to this question in both their teacher and their rock pupil voices.

Placing themselves in their rock pupil's shoes allowed teachers to view the situation through the eyes of a student with needs very different from their own. Additionally, it opened opportunities for teachers to become aware of how to plan for multiple forms of representation, engagement, and assessment that align with the learning needs of their students.

CREATING A TOUCHSTONE OF LEARNING

When students returned from Field Experience 1, they reviewed and consolidated their understandings of teaching and learning and their roles and identities as teachers by once again engaging with their rock companions.

During class, teachers individually and silently designed a 3-D rock/pebble visual that represented a crucial learning from their first encounter with students and schools, and afterward submitted a two-hundred-word excerpt along with a photo or drawing that metaphorically represented memorable learning. Some of the submissions were pictures of mountains and rocks, metaphors for inherent strengths such as courage and love. Other students included poems or pictures depicting themes related to a deepening appreciation for diversity and complexity of the teaching process, as well as their students and colleagues.

The excerpts were then gathered into an e-book, which was available for viewing by students, as well as the faculty and the staff. This provided a platform for students to share their personal and professional insights as new teachers—their voices of wisdom, nurtured by their contemplative interactions with the rocks. This activity allowed students to capture and savor a persistent image related to an important aspect of teaching and learning, as well as the teacher self, that would always be accessible, like a favorite rock in the pocket, a touchstone, that reminded them of what needed to be carried in their hearts and classrooms.

COMING FULL CIRCLE: MESSENGER ROCKS

At the end of the pragmatics course, students engaged with messenger rocks to bring their learning full circle. Students chose one rock from a collection and then contemplated upon the features of the rock they found attractive, as well as the potential message this rock might have for them in regard to their roles and identities as teachers. Afterward, students wrote a letter to their future teacher selves to remind them of the wisdom they received from their messenger rock. The letters were placed in a self-addressed envelope, sealed, and handed in. Students were assured that within a year's time, they would receive their letters that contained the worthy reminder from their messenger rock.

This activity was chosen to further invite an ongoing process of contemplative practice as preservice teachers continued to reimagine and live into their present and future selves as teachers. They were encouraged to create a practice of revisiting their messenger rocks from time to time and contemplate upon how well they are living into their preferred visions of self and role—deeply listening for any new insights or questions their messenger rock might have for them:

> If a rock could talk, what would it say. . . . Look up, look down, look all around!
> If a rock could talk, what would it say? It might ask you a question! (Hunter, n.d., p. 11).

THE PROF WITH THE BAG OF ROCKS

It takes courage to walk around campus with a bag of rocks. Sometimes people look wide-eyed after an affirmative response to their half joking query: "Wow that looks heavy. . . . What's in the bag? Rocks?" After the initial surprise subsides, the conversation usually shifts to the question of—why rocks?

Rocks as contemplative tools have the exceptional ability to engender authentic opportunities to explore awareness and wisdom that transform teachers and their practice. Using rocks in a teacher preparation course provided a tangible process for preservice teachers to physically and psychologically connect their inner and outer worlds, which enhanced their abilities to engage with diverse learners and be attentive to their students' inner and outer worlds.

The rocks supported contemplative opportunities that also facilitated self-reflection, collaboration, perspective taking, diversity awareness, creativity, and inspiration. Beholding and holding rocks is akin to treasuring the inner lives, voices, and integrity of preservice teachers who can make a difference by encouraging the song of the self to be seen, and bubble outward freely without fear, and to pass this courage onto their students—one rock at a time.

ESSENTIAL IDEAS TO CONSIDER

- Utilizing a physical touchstone such as a rock supports contemplative and reflective processes in teaching and learning by grounding and joining the present moment and one's experiences, allowing deeper learning and insights to emerge.
- Rocks are an engaging metaphor for the stable yet changing nature of the self. Thus, used as a contemplative tool, rocks support insight into the complex interactions and changes that take place between self and role when becoming a teacher.
- Rocks invite preservice teachers to contemplate the inner and outer aspects of teaching and learning in an accessible and safe manner, particularly when exploring potentially sensitive topics such as diversity, perspective taking, and self-awareness.
- Used as a collaboration tool, rocks support the interactive knowledge building and sharing process that is essential to reaping wisdom in teaching and learning through contemplative social processes.

REFERENCES

Benson, P. (2008). Sparks: How parents can help ignite the hidden strengths of teenagers. San Francisco: Jossey-Bass.

Brown, B. (2012). *Daring greatly: How the courage to be vulnerable transforms the way we live, love, parent, and lead.* New York: Avery.

Center for Contemplative Mind in Society. (2015). What are contemplative practices? Retrieved from http://www.contemplativemind.org/practices.

Clandinin, D. J., Schaefer, L., Long, J. S., Steeves, P., Mckenzie-Robblee, S., Pinnegar, E., . . . Downey, C. A. (2012). *Early career teacher attrition: Problems, possibilities, potentials; Final report.* Edmonton, AB: Centre for Research for Teacher Education and Development, University of Alberta.

Collins, S., & Arthur, N. (2010). Self-awareness and awareness of client cultural identities. In N. Arthur & S. Collins (Eds.), *Culture-infused counselling* (2nd ed., pp. 67–102). Calgary, AB: Counselling Concept.

Hart, T. (2004). Opening the contemplative mind in the classroom. *Journal of Transformative Education, 2*(1), 28–46. doi:10.1177/1541344603259311.

Hunter, E. (n.d.). If a rock could talk, what would it say? In *K–3 integrated resource unit: Kids and rocks*. Vancouver, BC: Mineralsed.

Jacobsen, M., Lock. J., & Friesen, S. (2013). Strategies for engagement: Knowledge building and intellectual engagement in participatory learning environments. *Education Canada, 53*(1). Retrieved from http://www.cea-ace.ca.

Kessler, R. (2000). *The soul of education: Helping students find connection, compassion, and character at school*. Alexandria, VA: Association for Supervision and Curriculum Development.

Krantz, L. (2006). *Only one you*. New York: Cooper Square.

Lydon, M. (1968, December). Carl Perkins. *Rolling Stone, 7*, 23. Retrieved from http://www.rocksbackpages.com.

Morton, N. (1977). *The journey is home*. Boston: Beacon.

Noordhoff, K. (2012). The power of paradox in learning to teach. *New Directions for Teaching and Learning* (130), 53–65. doi:10.1002/tl.20017.

O'Reilley, M. R. (1998). *Radical presence: Teaching as contemplative practice*. Portsmouth, NH: Heinemann.

Palmer, P. J. (1998). *The courage to teach: Exploring the inner landscape of a teacher's life*. San Francisco: Jossey-Bass.

Palmer, P., & Zajonc, A. (2010). *The heart of higher education*. San Francisco: Jossey-Bass.

Poutiatine, M. I., & Conners, D. A. (2012). The role of identity in transformational learning, teaching, and leading. *New Directions for Teaching and Learning, 212* (130), 67–75. doi:10.1002/tl.20018.

Chapter Three

Reframing How We Think About Learning

A Four-Source Model

Kristin N. Rainville, Sacred Heart University, Fairfield, Connecticut;
Katie Egan Cunningham, Manhattanville College, Purchase, New York

Central to our work as teacher educators focused on literacy and leadership are the ways we position the learning process as contemplative in nature. Daniel Barbezat and Mirabai Bush (2014) define contemplative approaches in higher education as the exploration of students' own beliefs and views through critical inquiry for the purpose of serving our common human future. They write, "Personal introspection and contemplation reveal our inextricable connection to each other, opening the heart and mind to true community, deeper insight, sustainable living, and a more just society" (p. vx).

To engage in personal introspection and to build learning communities with one another, our students are asked to share who they are, where they are from, and what matters most to them. They engage in disciplined and guided self-reflection. They are asked to bridge theory with practice and to have the courage to feel things deeply as they reflect on their own education. Through this process our students take notice of the multiple sources we learn from and they are supported to view the learning process itself from a place of gratitude.

In this chapter, we describe a framework we have applied in our work with preservice teacher candidates using the Sanskrit shloka, or poetic verse, that describes learning as originating through four sources that can be translated as learning from one's teacher, oneself, one's peers, and with time. Shlokas are Hindu prayers grounded in spirituality. In the next section, we explain the teaching and learning context that fuels this work. In subsequent sections, we explain the four-source framework and detail the practical engagements to emphasize a particular source of learning as we intentionally support our students in their path toward becoming teachers.

TEACHING AND LEARNING CONTEXT

Teacher candidates are entering the field at a time of significant change due to increased accountability measures including new teacher certification requirements, new high-stakes tests, and other evolving mandated assessments. Rigorous teacher evaluations, increased standardization including the Common Core State Standards, scripted curriculum, oftentimes competing initiatives at the school level, and the politicization of public schools are just a few of the ongoing changes in teacher education.

Additionally, America's classrooms are increasingly diverse. Forty-eight percent of P–12 students are students of color (National Center for Education Statistics, 2012), and 20 percent come from homes where native languages other than English are spoken (U.S. Census Bureau, 2001).

As K–12 schools experience these sweeping changes, institutions of teacher education are encountering their own changes with the implementation of national standards set forth by the Council of Accreditation of Educator Preparation (CAEP) and increased oversight and reporting by state agencies. In response to these changes, through observational and direct teaching experiences, our teacher candidates are asked to draw on their own interpretations of what they witness in schools, to disrupt practices that overemphasize goals over process, to instead focus on the relationships of students to what they are learning, to the world, and to one another.

CONCEPTUAL FRAMEWORK

In response to the teaching and learning environments in K–12 schools and with recognition of the shifting demographics in our suburban areas that indicate an increasingly culturally and linguistically diverse population, we have designed programs that are culturally responsive (Moll, Amanti, Neff, & Gonzalez, 1992) and grounded in a belief that learning is socially situated and context specific (Lewis, 2001). In doing so, we also draw from John Dewey's (1933) belief that effective teachers need to possess three characteristics in addition to knowledge and skills in order to be effective: open-mindedness, wholeheartedness, and intellectual reasonability.

Dewey's emphasis on teachers' dispositional stances can be further understood as demonstrating empathy, caring, reflection, and willingness to adjust. As Dennis Shirley and Elizabeth MacDonald (2016) explain, "The important of open-mindedness, commitment to the whole child, and educators as lifelong learners—the cornerstones of Dewey's philosophy—are reflected in mindful teaching" (p. 75).

Inspired by the work of Dewey, contemplative practices in higher education place students at the center of their own learning (Bush, 2011). Although Dewey did not write about mindfulness in particular, his work has laid a foundation for the relationship among awareness, reflection, and action in everyday living (Hyde & LaPrad, 2015).

In addition to supporting students with pedagogical methods, we recognize that we have an impact on their evolving beliefs about what it means to be a teacher. In this way, we draw from Paulo Freire (1992/2014) and bell hooks's (2003) concepts of a pedagogy of hope as well as the concept of educators as agents of change (Ayers, Kumashiro, Meiners, Quinn, & Stovall, 2010). A contemplative framework includes compassion, which helps moves us to the relief of suffering, which is also aligned with a pedagogy of hope and social change (Hyde & LaPrad, 2015; Jones & Rainville, 2014).

FOUR SOURCE MODEL FOR LEARNING AND GROWING

The Sanskrit shloka that describes learning as four sources for how we learn and grow reads as follows:

AchAryAt pAdamAdatte, pAdam shiShyaH swamedhayA |
sa-brahmachAribhyaH pAdam, pAdam kAlakrameNa cha || (Practical Sanskrit, 2009)

This shloka can be translated as learning from one's teacher, oneself, one's peers, and with time. These four sources help guide our collaborative thinking, planning, and teaching as we strive to place our students at the center of our work.

The four-source model for learning and growing requires continuous, disciplined reflection. The following sections detail specific course engagements that emphasize a particular source and the impact these practices have had on our preservice teacher candidates. While in this chapter we purposefully align particular engagements under specific sources, many engagements draw from multiple sources simultaneously.

SOURCE ONE: FROM TEACHER

It is the first class of the new semester. Few candidates are chatting with each other, a signal that they have not had classes together before and that they are not familiar with each other. Before we get to the syllabus and the expectations of the course, we listen to George Ella Lyon (1999) read her powerful poem "Where I'm From." Everyone is prompted to compose their own "Where I'm From" poem. Uncertainty and apprehension is evident as students dig in to writing about themselves, surrounded by strangers, connected by only perhaps the same goal of becoming a teacher.

After several minutes of writing, the candidates are prompted to reread their poem and choose one line from their poem to share. As the teachers, we ensure that we take that first risk and "go first" by adding a line from our own poems. By doing so, we are modeling vulnerability as we share a part of ourselves beyond the identity of teacher and discuss the importance of this if we are expecting students to share a piece of themselves.

When candidates are ready, each person comes up and adds their line to the class poem we are creating. When the poem is crafted we each read aloud our own line. The following is a sample poem created in one of our sections:

> I am from the game players, learn and follow the rules and get ahead.
> I am from Ukrainian and Italian traditions with hand-made babka bread and perogies.
> I am from the silverware drawer where butter knives pose as screwdrivers.
> I am from respect, giving and receiving at all times.
> I am from the city that never sleeps where thousands of people walk the streets.

At the end of the reading, the candidates are thanked for their willingness to share parts of themselves. This shared writing is the first experience that candidates have of the teacher modeling gratitude and compassion for our students.

As Hilary Conklin (2008) argued, rather than blame prospective teachers for the experiences they have or have not had, teacher educators must come to know and honor the experiences that teacher candidates bring to the classroom and use these experiences as a starting point for learning. As Thich Nhat Hanh (1993) explains,

> When we grow a lemon tree, we want it to be vigorous and beautiful. But, if it isn't vigorous and beautiful, we don't blame the tree. We observe it in order to understand why it isn't growing well. Perhaps we have not taken good care of it. We know it is funny to blame a lemon tree, but we do blame human beings when they are not growing well; human beings are not very different from lemon trees. If we take good care of them, they will grow properly. Blaming never helps. Only love and understanding can help people change. (pp. 30–31)

In addition to capitalizing on candidates' lived experiences, we also share our beliefs, stories, and journeys as teachers and learners. For example, table 3.1 lists some of our core beliefs as teachers and teacher educators and how those beliefs come to life in our courses. By making our core beliefs explicit and modeling how they come to life in our classrooms, we are demonstrating how teachers can carry out their central beliefs every day by embodying their practice. This involves attending to the present pedagogical moment, knowing one's students, and being mindful of how these elements interact with the content (Hyde & LaPrade, 2015; Jones & Rainville, 2014).

SOURCE TWO: FROM SELF

"Settle down, it'll all be clear / Don't pay no mind to the demons / They fill you with fear / The trouble—it might drag you down / If you get lost, you can always be found" (Holden & Pearson, 2012). The lyrics to "Home," sung by Phillip Phillips, are played against a black screen until the first slide of Teresa's digital story appeared.

In this slide, Teresa (all names are pseudonyms) is held by a figure of a man with the stark text "1968–1998." As Teresa's digital story continued, we learned about the ways she pays daily tribute to the good man her father was

Table 3.1.   Beliefs and examples

Belief	Example
Teachers are lifelong learners.	We share our own reading and writing plans if we ask our candidates to do the same.
Teachers must be willing to take risks.	We share video clips of ourselves teaching young children to model specific practices.
Teachers can come to recognize their own vulnerabilities.	We are willing to say I don't know or to cry when so moved.
Teachers learn from listening to others.	We are listeners who learn from our students' experiences and let them know it.
Teachers learn from differing perspectives.	We are clear and vocal about our belief systems and model that each session. The intention is not to recruit students toward a liberal bias but rather to come to understand their own evolving beliefs more deeply.
Teachers see potential for learning in all life's experiences.	We weave stories from learning throughout our lives in our teaching.

and how his memory influences her as a teacher today. We see the ways her family and friends are the pillars she leans on. In the end, she explains that she has realized through the process of composing her digital story that in her role as teacher she is never alone.

The digital story project is designed to support candidates to tell the story of who they want to be as teachers. In crafting her digital story, Teresa went through a series of guided exercises to better understand her multiple identities as a teacher, student, daughter, and friend. Through this process, she had to make choices about what to reveal and what to hide.

One of the goals of the digital story writing process is for candidates to gain a sense of worthiness through contemplation. As Brené Brown (2010) writes, "Authenticity is a collection of choices that we have to make every day. It's about the choice to show up and be real. The choice to be honest. The choice to let our true selves be seen" (p. 49). Our program embraces a pedagogy of vulnerability as part of the contemplative process. A pedagogy of vulnerability is diametrically opposed to what teachers are often asked to do, that is, to be all knowing. A pedagogy of vulnerability risks exposing ourselves to others but also frees us to reveal uncertainty.

In coming to make choices about their digital stories, preservice teacher candidates are asked to make decisions about themselves. They begin by mind mapping the multiple identities and roles they have using a process of visual diagrams to show the relationships between ideas and information. They continue to map with a focus on the myriad ways they visualize and conceptualize their teacher self, such as teacher as storybook changed by her students' stories; teacher as compass serving as a constant and reliable north; and teacher as lighthouse, guiding safe passage through the learning journey.

Candidates then engage in a series of story-mapping exercises that ask them to plan for the images, text, and sounds that will compose the story they are telling about their teacher identities. Through the writing process, candidates begin to view identity as performative and shifting. They begin to critically embrace the idea that there is no singular self. Rather, through the decision-making process, they come to recognize that we bring multiple identities to the classroom depending on where we are, who we are with, and what our intentions are in that moment. Through this iterative process of self-reflection and composition, they also come to recognize that there is no singular teacher identity.

SOURCE THREE: FROM PEERS

While watching a video clip of a peer teaching, Don (a teacher candidate) responded, "The way that the teacher pulled the students back in was good; I liked it." Although encouraging, this feedback included a judgment (that the teaching move was "good" and that Don "liked it") and would not provide his peer with specific enough guidance on what was good and why it was good.

In order to support preservice and in-service teachers to become more comfortable with both observing their peers and providing and receiving feedback, we structure methods courses in ways that scaffold candidates to become mindful participants in peer coaching. A framework that has been beneficial for candidates in this process is the "See, Think, Wonder" routine, adopted from Harvard's Project Zero (Harvard Graduate School of Education, 2009). This framework helps candidates to move from the descriptive to the analytical and potentially transformative without making judgments using three prompts:

- What do you see? (I see)
- What does this make you think about? (I think)
- What does it make you wonder? (I wonder)

Nonjudgment is at the heart of both mindfulness and peer coaching. Candidates are supported to distinguish the difference between observation and interpretation (or between recalling and describing). Next, candidates are asked to become aware of and acknowledge their interpretation (judging thought) and then, if possible, reframe the interpretation as a nonjudgmental question, or a wondering. This is accomplished by watching short video clips of one another teaching.

The first viewing of the teaching video occurs without a prompt; candidates watch the video and then talk with a partner about what they saw. Before the second viewing, the "see, think, wonder" framework is introduced and candidates are asked to use this framework as a lens to observe teaching.

During the second viewing, Don used the "see, think, wonder" framework to be more mindful and specific in his observations. Don's revised feedback was as follows:

> I noticed that when you reread the last line of the of the page you read aloud before the turn and talk, that students were cued to finish their sentence and every student was listening by the time you read the first sentence on the new page. I am wondering how students knew to do that and because I think that is a more effective strategy for managing the turn and talk rather than counting or clapping, which is not only jarring to students but does not always work for me.

By using the see-think-wonder framework to guide his observation and share with his peers, Don was able to be more specific about the management strategy he observed and the positive effect the strategy had in the classroom. Not only does the peer receive thoughtful feedback, but also Don was able to articulate the specific teaching strategy he saw in a teaching video, which could potentially transform his own practice.

In addition to Don's learning, the group came to the conclusion that there is nothing wrong with having an opinion, but it is important to notice if there is a sense of righteousness that comes along with it. If feedback comes with judgment or with righteousness, peers will not be as open to suggestions or willing to work with one another.

SOURCE FOUR: WITH TIME

Melissa, a career changer and graduate student, was in her last semester of her master's degree program. Melissa had many experiences in schools as a teacher's aide but was now seeking certification toward having her own classroom. In the beginning of the course, she expressed that she never thought of teachers as leaders. Rather, she felt her role was to implement lessons according to a predetermined curriculum. By the end of the course, she was beginning to define her role as teacher in new ways including leader, researcher, and curriculum creator.

In addition, she was openly sharing her self-perceived strengths, challenges, fears, and daily attempts to redefine herself as a leader. For example, when Melissa volunteered to go first in a class discussion, she first explained, "Today, I am trying to follow the philosophy of go first. I am not a risk taker, but I am going first now. This is hard for me." She was redefining her concept of teacher as well as the ways she thought about herself.

Unlike Melissa, Beth was new to education. As an undergraduate, she was being introduced to pedagogical methods and coming to understand school culture no longer as a student but as an aspiring teacher. In a field-based literacy methods course, Beth worked with a small group of culturally and linguistically diverse elementary school students who were predominantly from working poor homes. After her first session with her new students, Beth cried to her peers about the contents of the young students' heart maps based on Georgia Heard's (1999) technique, which revealed identities and childhoods very different from her own.

Heartmapping is an arts method of drawing or collaging the contents of one's heart including important people, places, and memories. As Beth continued working alongside students over the length of a semester, she began to reposition her own vulnerability and the vulnerability of her students not as a source of despair or shame but as the birthplace of joy, creativity, hope, and change. She also spoke of the critical recognition of valuing what we do not know as teachers, particularly when it comes to students, to shift their view of time to a stance that embraces time through presence and patience.

We cannot control time; however, we can control how we, as individuals, frame our core beliefs and vision for our students including creating lifelong learners and situating the classroom as a "location of possibility" (hooks, 1994, p. 107).

To help teacher candidates see how this stance is enacted in practice, they are supported to recognize changes they see in themselves and in their perceptions of students that come with time. We also continuously model these practices. As Thich Nhat Hanh (2007) reflects,

> To dwell in the here and now does not mean you never think about the past or responsibly plan for the future. The idea is simply not to allow yourself to get lost in regrets about the past or worries about the future. If you are firmly grounded in the present moment, the past can be an object of inquiry, the object of your mindfulness and concentration. You can attain many insights by looking into the past. But you are still grounded in the present moment. (p. 128)

CONCLUSION

There remains work to be done. While we have been applying this four-source model as an inspiration for the engagements we design in our programs, we have also come to recognize that we can be more explicit with our teacher candidates about what we have learned about the four sources of learning and how the framework itself can provide them with a touchstone for their own practice. Our hope is that our students will in turn bring contemplative modes of instruction into their own classrooms by finding out who their students are, where they are from, and how they can bring compassion, reflection, and inquiry into the heart of the learning experiences they create with their students.

ESSENTIAL IDEAS TO CONSIDER

- The Sanskrit shloka that describes learning as four sources for how we learn and grow can be used to build contemplative practices into teacher education programs.
- Teacher educators can model their own compassion, personal introspection, and inquiry to support teacher candidates through contemplative practices.
- Recognition of one's own vulnerability is central to how we learn and grow.

REFERENCES

Ayers, W., Kumashiro, K., Meiners, E., Quinn, T., & Stovall, D. (2010). *Teaching towards democracy: Educators as agents of change.* Boulder, CO: Paradigm.

Barbezat, D. P., & Bush, M. (2014). *Contemplative practices in higher education: Powerful methods to transform teaching and learning.* San Francisco: Jossey-Bass.

Brown, B. (2010). *The gifts of imperfection: Let go of who you think you're supposed to be and embrace who you are.* Center City, MN: Hazelden.

Bush, M. (2011). Mindfulness in higher education. *Contemporary Buddhism, 12*(1). doi:10.1080/14639947.2011.5648838.

Conklin, H. G. (2008). Modeling compassion in critical justice-oriented teacher education. *Harvard Educational Review, 78*(4), 652–674.

Dewey, J. (1933). *How we think.* Buffalo, NY: Prometheus.

Freire, P. (1992/2014). *Pedagogy of hope: Reliving pedagogy of the oppressed.* New York: Bloomsbury.

Hanh, T. N. (1993). *Interbeing: Fourteen guidelines for engaged Buddhism.* Berkeley, CA: Paralax.

Hanh, T. N. (2007). *The art of power.* New York: Harper One.

Harvard Graduate School of Education. (2009). Visible thinking. Retrieved April 30, 2016, from http://www.pz.harvard.edu.

Heard, G. (1999). *Awakening the heart: Exploring poetry in elementary and middle school.* Portsmouth, NH: Heinemann.

Holden, G., & Pearson, D. (2012). Home. [Recorded by P. Phillips]. *The world from the side of the moon* [Digital Download]. Burbank, CA: Interscope Records.

hooks, b. (1994). *Teaching to transgress: Education as the practice of freedom.* New York: Routledge.

hooks, b. (2003). *Teaching community: A pedagogy of hope.* New York: Routledge.

Hyde, A. M., & LaPrad, J. G. (2015). Mindfulness, democracy, and education. *Democracy and Education, 23*(2), 1–12.

Jones, S., & Rainville, K. N. (2014). Flowing with resistance: Suffering, humility, and compassion in literacy coaching. *Reading and Writing Quarterly: Overcoming Learning Disabilities, 30*(3), 270–287.

Lewis, C. (2001). *Literacy practices as social acts: Power, status, and cultural norms in the classroom.* New York: Routledge.

Lyon, G. E. (1999). *Where I'm from, where poems come from.* Spring, TX: Absey.

Moll, L. C., Amanti, C., Neff, D., & Gonzalez, N. (1992). Funds of knowledge for teaching: Using a qualitative approach to connect homes and classrooms. *Theory into Practice, 31*(2), 132–141.

National Center for Education Statistics. (2012). *Digest of education statistics*, table 44. Washington, DC: U.S. Department of Education.

Practical Sanskrit. (2009). How we learn and grow. *Om! This is Sanskrit* (blog). Retrieved from http://blog.practicalsanskrit.com.

Shirley, D., & MacDonald, E. (2016). *The mindful teacher.* New York: Teachers College Press.

United States Census Bureau. (2001). *Population 5 years and over who spoke a language other than English at home by language group and English-speaking ability.* Appendix Table 1. Retrieved from http://www.census.gov/hhes/socdemo/language/data/acs/ACS-12.pdf.

Chapter Four

Using Contemplative Pedagogies to Explore Diversity within and beyond One's Experience in Preservice Teacher Education

Jeremy Forest Price, Indiana University–Purdue University Indianapolis (IUPUI), Indianapolis, Indiana

Beyond the complex amalgamation of content, process, and context goals of teacher education, many teacher education programs are deliberately informed by the desire to build an inclusive society in an increasingly diverse world. As the K–12 student population in the United States is becoming more diverse (National Center for Educational Statistics [NCES], 2013), research has demonstrated that the mostly white, middle-class undergraduates who self-select to become teachers have struggled to effectively meet the needs of and form effective pedagogical relationships with the heterogeneous students that populate their classrooms (Grossman & McDonald, 2008; Lowenstein, 2009).

This disconnect likely contributes to disparities in national measures of academic achievement (NCES, 2013). One effective approach to helping educators develop the dispositions and critical awareness to foster inclusive and culturally responsive classrooms is by engaging teachers and teacher candidates in deep identity work to recognize their own positionality and place in a diverse cultural milieu (Jupp, Berry, & Lensmire, 2016; Lowenstein, 2009; Utt & Tochluck, 2016).

Contemplative pedagogies in particular provide a grounded practice for designing learning opportunities for undergraduate teacher candidates to deeply explore and prepare to face these urgent and challenging core issues of educational equity in contemporary times. With an emphasis on deliberative self-awareness and attention and the intentional goals of developing open-mindedness, living with paradox, and encouraging civic engagement (Burggraf & Grossenbacher, 2007), contemplative pedagogies can foster learning experiences that encourage future teachers to become more effective and inclusive educators by approaching each educational situation and relationship in its own context and on its own merits.

This chapter describes the efforts undertaken at a regional comprehensive university in West Virginia in central Appalachia to support the development of an inclusive mindset and critical consciousness through contemplative pedagogies with teacher candidates. In this predominantly rural Appalachian state, the prevailing narrative from inside and out is that the population is homogeneous and monolithic in terms of characteristics and outlook despite evidence to the contrary (Barlow, 2014; Pollard, 2004).

Historically and in modern times, terms such as "hillbilly" and "redneck" have been applied to the residents of the Appalachian region, reinforcing the narrative of a backward, isolated, and intolerant people (Barlow, 2014; Lilly & Todd, 2015). The term "redneck" may have come from West Virginia (Lilly & Todd, 2015). Historically, it was a badge of solidarity among organized coal mine workers from around the world who wore red bandannas around their neck working in the Blair Mountain mines.

The workers rose up against the coal companies to demand better—and less dangerous—working conditions, better pay, and freedom from company scrip. The confrontation turned violent, and the workers' demands remained unmet. "Redneck" is a term that arose from the quest for solidarity and social justice yet has been misappropriated, starting with the mine owners as a form of publicity damage control, to describe people who are backward, stubborn, and poor. The course work described in this chapter was oriented toward recognizing and redefining narratives that are potentially applied to teacher candidates and their future students—particularly with respect to the term "redneck"—through contemplative and mindful inquiry practices (Barbezat & Bush, 2014; Burggraf & Grossenbacher, 2007).

The teacher candidates are keenly aware of the ways that the people in the state and the region are portrayed, as poverty stricken, drug addicted, tattoo covered, overweight, and living in trailers (Kristoff, 2014). The teacher candidates are concerned that these depictions serve as the way that outsiders see their region and that these representations serve to dehumanize the successes and struggles experienced by individuals of Appalachia.

By engaging in contemplative and mindful inquiry practices, students learned to speak for and define themselves, recognize the voices and uniqueness of others, value this interplay of diversity, and transcend the narratives that have been spun to constrain their interactions. In doing so, the aim was to further allow them to recognize the narratives that they may unintentionally apply to others, especially the students they will eventually teach.

COURSE CONTEXT

Contemplative pedagogies were integrated into a one-credit elective course (two one-hour sessions per week for eight weeks) intended for undergraduate teacher education students and entitled Social and Emotional Approaches to Teaching and Learning. Students enrolled in the course were undergraduate teacher education majors in the School of Education at a public comprehensive university in the predominantly rural state of West Virginia. The university they attended largely serves individuals emerging from families with no prior college experience, the working class, and veterans.

This range of backgrounds, experiences, and situations is mirrored in these students. The thirteen elementary teacher candidates enrolled in the course were in various stages of their teacher preparation pathway, from preadmissions to the semester prior to student teaching. The students were self-selected and motivated for this elective course, approved originally to provide teacher education course work while preparing to enter the teacher education program. Teacher candidates who had already been accepted into the program also enrolled in the course, seeking course work that would extend their understandings of teaching beyond the prescribed core curriculum.

The course was organized into four overarching units: (1) Introducing Social and Emotional Approaches to Teaching and Learning; (2) The Impact of Stories on Teaching and Learning; (3) Your Work to Model Social and Emotional Approaches; and (4) Social and Emotional Teaching and Learning in the Wide World.

The focus of this effort to incorporate and model contemplative pedagogies in service of inclusive teaching centered on two sequential units that formed the middle core of the four-unit course. Unit 2, The Impact of Stories on Teaching and Learning, explored the idea that the stories we tell about ourselves and others influence the attitudes and values that we bring to our teaching and learning experiences. Unit 3, Your Work to Model Social and Emotional Approaches, focused on the importance of modeling by educators of introspection, contemplative and deliberative practices, and identity work for K–12 students.

THE ROLE OF CONTEMPLATIVE PRACTICES AND PEDAGOGY

Contemplative pedagogy served to allow the students in the course, most of whom will stay and teach in the region, to recognize the narratives that are told about others, about themselves, and about the people in their state and the Appalachian region.

With a focus on self-awareness, open-mindedness, and deliberative action, contemplative pedagogical practices provided opportunities to engage with the concepts of prejudice and preordained narratives, poverty, race, and dialect in a mindful manner where outward behaviors are considered and matched with intents. Elizabeth MacDonald and Dennis Shirley (2009), while referring more generally to the chaotic life of the classroom, point to the idea that missing a mindful approach to teaching and learning can lead to actions that may be regretted later, especially when considering the complex layers of diversity in the relationships between students and teachers.

I used the framework developed by Susan Burggraf and Peter Grossenbacher (2007) to organize the contemplative activities into modes. The contemplative course activities were aligned with the following modes and were experienced by the teacher candidates in the course in the following order:

- *reflective reading*: attentive engagement with the visual arts, such as recognizing one's responses to a painting through aesthetic, dialogic, and written responses;
- *suspending judgment and assumptions*: careful listening while recognizing one's own preconceptions, such as engaging in a deliberate dialogue around a difficult issue;
- *contemplative reading*: nuanced and structured deep engagement with texts, such as a structured reading of and dialogue on a poem; and
- *cultivating compassion*: perspective taking and learning to value diversity, such as activities to explore one's social position in relation to others.

Each mode was represented by at least one activity in the course, described in detail in the following section. Each activity was based on particular contemplative pedagogies and practices advanced by authors such as Burggraf and Grossenbacher (2007), Daniel Barbezat and Mirabai Bush (2014), and Arthur Zajonc (2009).

The order of these modes was decided upon according to the sequence of understanding goals for the unit and the course as a whole. Students engaged in reflective reading first, for example, in order to begin a mindful exploration of ideas related to race and education in a relatively low-risk manner because they were not directly involved, which then led into a mindful listening exercise concerning an event in which they were an observer, and then a deeper mindful process of looking at themselves in relation to their community, the region, and the nation as a whole. The goals and protocols for each of these activities were distributed to the teacher candidates with encouragement to incorporate these pedagogical practices into their future teaching.

DESCRIPTION OF CONTEMPLATIVE ACTIVITIES

The contemplative activities were structured in order to build on one another and to encourage deeper practice over time. They were sequenced based on a progression of understanding, inquiry, and self-exploration, particularly around issues of racial, class-based, and regional identity.

Mindful Noticing: Contemplative Reading of Artwork

The "Mindful Noticing" activity (Barbezat & Bush, 2014), a type of reflective reading (Burggraf & Grossenbacher, 2007), was designed to help students recognize their responses to and reflect on the meanings portrayed by a work of visual art.

In order to help the teacher candidates start to explore issues of race and schooling, the painting *The Problem We All Live With* by Norman Rockwell (1964) was selected for this activity. This painting was inspired by the story of Ruby Bridges as she was escorted by U.S. Marshals to a court-ordered integrated school in New Orleans in 1960 (Gallagher & Zagacki, 2005). Behind Ruby, who is wearing a white dress and flanked by four U.S. Marshals in suits and official-looking yellow armbands, there are the remains of a tomato thrown against a wall scrawled with derogatory graffiti.

Adapted from a structure developed by Zajonc (2009), the students were guided through the following experience in relation to Rockwell's iconic painting:

- Take in the painting as a whole, without judging or evaluating your thoughts.
- Focus on one detail, big or small, without judging and evaluating your thoughts.
- Start noticing the words that you associate with the detail, picture these words, and hold on to these words.
- Take in the painting as a whole again, and then write down the words you associated with the detail in the painting.

Students then shared what they noticed with the class as a whole. These observations were written on the whiteboard in the front of the room and then discussed as a class. Students noticed and focused on a range of details in the painting, as detailed in table 4.1, including the paper in the pocket of a U.S. Marshal, the "n-word" graffiti scrawled on the wall, and Ruby Bridges's white dress. In addition to recognizing the more poignant details of the painting, the students also highlighted a number of tensions, such as attributing both "fear" and "fearless" to Ruby.

Table 4.1. Students' noticed details and the associations they shared from the painting *The Problem We All Live With* by Norman Rockwell

Detail	Associations
Girl	Willpower; determined; fearless; fear
"N-word"	Racism; inequality; hate; painful; judgment; worst word in the world, never say it
Paper in Marshal's pocket	What was it? courage; contempt
Tomato	Hate; anger; destruction; frustration; misunderstood; harmful; harassing; idiotic; fear
White dress	White; looks nice; braid and bow
Yellow band on Marshal's arm	Change; making a difference; protection

The process also raised further questions, such as the nature of the paper in the marshal's pocket. It could serve to humanize him if it is, as the students surmised, a photograph. Its presence also seems to have raised concerns: it may be his orders, demonstrating that he is protecting Ruby only because he is being told to do so. Through this contemplative activity, the teacher candidates began the process of unpacking and recognizing the range of schooling experiences based on ethnicity, race, and identity that may be different from their own.

Mindful Dialogue

The Mindful Dialogue activity was an opportunity for students to learn to suspend their assumptions and judgment (Burggraf & Grossenbacher, 2007). Based on the mindful listening activity outlined by Barbezat and Bush (2014, pp. 144–145), students were assigned to pairs and were given three minutes each to respond to the prompt: "Relate a time when you witnessed someone being treated differently because they were different." Following the structure developed by Barbezat and Bush, one student related her experience while the other student listened carefully without speaking. The listener then retold what he heard as accurately as he could; the speaker was encouraged to offer suggestions to the retelling.

The students then switched roles and repeated the process. As a class, the students shared some of the insights learned through the process. Many students related events dealing with race and class in their high schools; one student who worked in a childcare setting related her experience of seeing an African American boy being referred for discipline more frequently than his white classmates.

This exercise was an opportunity for students to learn to relate their experiences and to listen deeply and mindfully. This process was challenging for some teacher candidates: some found it difficult to fill the three minutes, and some found it difficult to suppress the urge to verbalize their responses to the speakers' stories.

All students, however, were able to use this activity as an opportunity to identify specific events in which they witnessed a prejudicial action against which they may have felt powerless to act or in which they did not necessarily recognize the significance of the event. The teacher candidates were able to engage in this activity in order to build a practice of deliberative self-awareness by recounting an event and attention by listening to their partner.

Privilege Walk

The students engaged in a "Privilege Walk" as a way to cultivate compassion (Burggraf & Grossenbacher, 2007) for those of whom, as Nicholas Kristof (2014) eloquently expressed, "even the starting line is out of reach." The Privilege Walk is an exercise in which participants learn to recognize their own positions of privilege in a concrete manner. They also learn to recognize the challenges that others encounter in negotiating everyday situations and events through a form of perspective taking by seeing explicitly how certain structural attributes can help certain people "get ahead" or keep others behind.

The structure of the activity was based on a standard protocol for Privilege Walks (Edewi, 2015). This activity encourages students to mindfully pay attention to their own positionality and to take on the perspectives of others. We lined up side by side holding hands.

As each prompt was read aloud—such as, "If your parents worked nights and weekends to support your family, take one step back" and "If you can show affection for your romantic partner in public without fear of ridicule or violence, take one step forward"—each individual in the class took a step back or forward. In order to fully participate in the activity, the teacher candidates had to deliberately consider their position in the social world. By the end of the exercise, we were in a staggered line.

Some students indicated in discussion that it was an eye-opening experience for them. Those students who were toward the back of the line indicated that they were surprised by their position; some of the students at the front of the staggered line were grateful for the luck of their position, while others had a difficult time participating in the discussion. In the exercise debrief, we discussed the ways we can be mindful of the different "starting lines" of students and the role that inequalities in terms of race, language, gender, socioeconomic status, religion, and ability plays in terms of where that starting line is in relation to others.

Contemplative Reading: Visiting and Revisiting Responses to the Poem "Appalachia"

We engaged in the contemplative reading practice of Lectio Divina to delve deeply into the meanings of a text in a nuanced manner and to recognize and call attention to one's own responses to the text (Barbezat & Bush, 2014; Burggraf & Grossenbacher, 2007).

This protocol provided a useful framework for experiencing the text and exploring the meanings that students brought to the text and provided an environment that "immerses students in the text so that they're swimming in it, even putting the snorkel beneath, rather than speed boating over the surface" (Barbezat & Bush, 2014, p. 115). The poem "Appalachia" by Muriel Miller Dressler (1973; textbox 4.1) was selected for this exercise as a way for the teacher candidates to engage in identity work and recognize that their experiences and cultural references have been chronicled in poetry.

Appalachia

I am Appalachia. In my veins
Runs fierce mountain pride; the hill-fed streams
Of passion; and, stranger, you don't know me!
You've analyzed my every move—you still
Go away shaking your head. I remain
Enigmatic. How can you find rapport with me—
You, who never stood in the bowels of hell,
Never felt a mountain shake and open its jaws
To partake of human sacrifice?
You, who never stood on a high mountain,
Watching the sun unwind its spiral rays;
Who never searched the glens for wild flowers,
Never picked mayapples or black walnuts; never ran
Wildly through the woods in pure delight,
Nor dangled your feet in a lazy creek?
You, who never danced to wild sweet notes,
Outpouring of nimble-fingered fiddlers;
Who never just "sat a spell," on a porch,
Chewing and whittling; or hearing in pastime
The deep-throated bay of chasing hounds
And hunters shouting with joy, "he's treed!"
You, who never once carried a coffin
To a family plot high up on a ridge
Because mountain folk know it's best to lie

Where breezes from the hills whisper, "you're home";
You, who never saw from the valley that graves on a hill
Bring easement of pain to those below?
I tell you, stranger, hill folk know
What life is all about; they don't need pills
To tranquilize the sorrow and joy of living.
I am Appalachia; and, stranger,
Though you've studied me, you still don't know.
                                    —Muriel Miller Dressler (1973)

Arranged in a circle of chairs, we followed an adapted version of the four-stage Lectio Divina protocol outlined by Barbezat and Bush (2014, p. 115). For each stage, each person in the class read one line of the poem until the entire poem was read aloud. Each teacher candidate then shared a reflection on the poem in turn. During the first stage—the first time the poem was read aloud—each teacher candidate shared his or her reactions to a particular word in the poem. The second stage increased the scope of reflection to a phrase in the poem, and for the third stage teacher candidates reflected on one or two lines in the poem. During the last stage we discussed the experience and the poem as a whole.

While sharing, many of the students remarked how this depiction of Appalachian life matched the stories their grandparents would tell them, and the students brought up the word "home" numerous times. This nostalgic twist was a strong indication of how much the region is an integral part of contemporary society while maintaining links to past generations.

During the readings, a student in the class from New England asked her classmates for help in interpreting some of the terms in the poem that were rooted in the local Appalachian dialect. While calling attention to their reactions to accounts of their own culture and traditions, they were able to engage in the type of self-exploration and identity work that is necessary for structuring inclusive and culturally responsive classrooms (Jupp, Berry, & Lensmire, 2016; Lowenstein, 2009; Utt & Tochluck, 2016).

The Redneck Redefinition Project Capstone Experience

The Redneck Redefinition Project was the capstone experience, intended as an opportunity for students to suspend their assumptions and judgment and cultivate compassion (Burggraf & Grossenbacher, 2007). Many of the students were sensitive to the way that Appalachia is cast in the popular imagination. Often this myth is framed by the term "redneck." One of the goals of this project was to allow the students in the class to reappropriate the term "redneck" in order to express the diversity and social values situated at the term's roots.

Each student was asked to create a design in which they

1. expressed their understanding of the stereotypical definition of redneck;
2. provided a redefinition of redneck, that is, how they would like to see the term defined based on their experiences and history; and
3. indicated why this redefinition is an important aspect of teaching and learning.

All students chose to create designs using Microsoft PowerPoint or Word, so these designs were printed on heat-transfer paper and ironed onto squares of red material to mirror the red bandanna origin of the term. The red squares were then sewn together into a quilt. Not only are quilts an effective way for presenting a mosaic of ideas, but also quilting as an art is aligned with the traditions and histories of Appalachian culture (Graff, 2012; Jarrell, 2009). Students also provided written reflections of the process, what they learned, and how their experiences changed their perspectives.

One particularly poignant panel design and written reflection can be found in figure 4.1 and textbox 4.2. This teacher candidate explored her background as a single mother from a family that experienced poverty and drug addiction and recognized that the derogatory use of the term "redneck" could very easily be applied to her. She pointed out this appellation would not be an accurate description of who she is and how she acts in the world. This teacher candidate, based on the recognition of her own situation, further vowed to be cognizant of and work against the effect of labels and prejudicial attitudes applied to her future students.

Figure 4.1.

A student's written reflection on the Redneck Redefinition Project

I stumbled across the "teach kids, not stereotypes" picture during a random Google search. I wanted to include it because it really sums up what the entire project means to me. It's about more than just rednecks; it's about all stereotypes and the way they shape our views and our interactions with each other. As a West Virginian, redneck is a stereotype I can identify with, so I can get a general idea of what it is like to be stereotyped; [this] gives me better insight to other groups and how they are stereotyped. As a teacher, I feel it is important to put those stereotypes that we hold for our students aside and teach the students without discrimination. I believe that if we are to stereotype the children, and treat them accordingly, then there's really no need for us to teach. In that case, we've already given them their story, the role they play in that story, and no way for them to write their own story.

I come from a low-income, white, West Virginian family. There are many substance abuse problems within my family tree. I'm also a single mother whose child does not know his father. Furthermore, I am also a recipient of various forms of government assistance in order to be able to buy food, see a doctor, have a place to live, afford childcare, and attend college. Many people could read that much about my life and make judgments or stereotype me. Unless they talked to me, they wouldn't know that I work hard, I'm a good mother, I'm going to college to better my chances for a good job in order to get off of government-assistance programs, or that I speak out strongly against drug use, child abuse, and taking advantage of government-assistance programs. I feel that the stereotypes I fall into mean I have to fight harder than some others in order to prove myself. I don't want to be the person putting that kind of pressure on my students when I am a teacher. I believe that encouraging children to know and love who they are is an important part of teaching.

Some of the students' work only scratched the surface of the history and meanings of the term "redneck," not delving into the social justice and search for solidarity origins of the term. These students redefined the phrase largely in terms of reclaiming a sense of pride rather than a sense of community. Other students placed a great deal of effort and contemplation into their designs and grappled fully with what "redneck" has come to mean in historical context. It is difficult to uncover and examine stereotypes, especially when they are aimed at oneself. The contemplative approach provided a framework for this identity work, but the courage and disposition to engage fully in the inquiry takes time and practice.

CONCLUSION AND LESSONS LEARNED

Through the contemplative pedagogies and activities in the course, students became more aware and mindful of the narratives, prejudicial discourse, and actions assigned to people because of their otherness. Some students not only recognized these narratives but also made deliberate efforts to ensure they do not unintentionally continue these harmful and denigrating moves.

One teacher candidate, for example, inspired by the mindful inquiry into issues of race and socioeconomic status in education, created a framework for bringing principles of restorative justice into his classroom. Another teacher candidate, the student from New England, recognized through her inquiry and self-examination that inequity and prejudice cuts across all regions of the nation and designed a lesson plan for engaging her students in inclusive and mindful practices.

Some of these students were able to engage in self-exploration and identity work to recognize the diversity of their region and history despite the monolithic narrative spun around them, and worked to recast and reframe these narratives in a way that was consistent with their experiences and history. Research has shown that engaging white, middle-class, dialectally neutral educators in the exploration of and inquiry into their own sense of identity is a critical step in helping them foster inclusive and responsive classrooms. The fact that even a small number of students uncovered this insight, requiring deep introspection and exploration of materials, is a testament to the potential power of contemplative pedagogical practices.

There were three main areas for future consideration: allocating sufficient time and space for practice, scaffolding and supporting deliberative action, and making the transition from finding voice to recognizing one's role in a full choir. For the first area, the course met for a total of only sixteen hours. Because of this time limitation, we merely skimmed the surface of a contemplative approach to identity work, compassion, and inclusivity. It would have been beneficial for the students to have the opportunity to engage in the contemplative pedagogical strategies on multiple occasions and develop these strategies into a full and meaningful practice.

Related to the necessity of time for practice is the necessity of providing appropriate scaffolding for supporting deliberative action. Deliberative action—recognizing the connections between intents and actions—as a mindful practice requires the time, modeling, feedback, and support necessary for the development of any practice. This inquiry highlighted the necessity and starting points of these supportive pedagogical and curricular structures in a mindful and contemplative approach to teaching and learning for preservice teachers.

In terms of the third area, many of the students were able to recognize through contemplative practices the power of finding their voice, particularly through the Redneck Redefinition Project. The intent, however, was to turn the power of voice into a recognition of and engagement with the human tendency to prejudge and spin narratives for others.

Only a small number of students took this next step, going beyond the content of the experience and recognizing the ways in which action could be taken, imagining themselves as teachers who can empower their future learners rather than just as students. Moving from understanding ideas and concepts as a student to putting a concrete plan into place as a future educator is a difficult step for many undergraduate teacher candidates. Most of the emphasis in designing this pilot course was put on the design of the activities; the next step is to develop the framework for scaffolding the transfer of understanding from learner in the higher education classroom to building concrete practices as a future educator.

Inequality, prejudice, and preordained narratives are at the heart of a number of challenges in K–12 education today. Grappling with these difficult and complex topics is necessary to ensure justice- and inclusion-seeking teachers. The contemplative approaches outlined in this chapter provided future educators with the opportunity to engage with these topics in a deep and mindful manner, setting the stage for teachers who recognize not only the stories that their students bring to the classroom but also a mindfulness of the stories their students have yet to tell.

ESSENTIAL IDEAS TO CONSIDER

- Contemplative pedagogical approaches helped students became more aware and mindful of the narratives, prejudicial discourse, and actions assigned to people because of their otherness.
- Some of these students were able to engage in self-exploration and identity work to recognize the diversity of their region and history despite the monolithic narrative spun around them, and worked to recast and reframe these narratives in a way that was consistent with their experiences and history.
- More work is needed to ensure that sufficient time and space for practice is allocated for sustained engagement and that scaffolding and supports are developed to encourage deliberative action and to make the transition from simply finding one's voice to recognizing one's role in a broader community of justice-seeking educators.

REFERENCES

Barbezat, D. P., & Bush, M. (2014). *Contemplative practices in higher education: Powerful methods to transform teaching and learning.* San Francisco: Jossey-Bass.

Barlow, A. (2014, May 12). The hillbilly divide. *Academe Blog.* Retrieved from http://academeblog.org.

Burggraf, S., & Grossenbacher, P. (2007). Contemplative modes of inquiry in liberal arts education. *LiberalArtsOnline.* Retrieved from http://www.wabash.edu.

Edewi, D. (2015, July 4). What is privilege. BuzzFeed. Retrieved from http://www.buzzfeed.com.

Gallagher, V., & Zagacki, K. S. (2005). Visibility and rhetoric: The power of visual images in Norman Rockwell's depictions of civil rights. *Quarterly Journal of Speech, 91*(2), 175–200.

Graff, E. R. (2012). Preserving traditional culture in the Cumberland Gap region. *Journal of Appalachian Studies, 18*(1/2), 234–243.

Grossman, P., & McDonald, M. (2008). Back to the future: Directions for research in teaching and teacher education. *American Educational Research Journal, 45*, 1, 184–205.

Jarrell, T. T. (2009). Quilts in Appalachia. Special Collections at Belk Library, Appalachian State University. Retrieved from http://collections.library.appstate.edu.

Jupp, J. C., Berry, T. R., & Lensmire, T. J. (2016). Second-wave white teacher identity studies: A review of white teacher identity literatures from 2004 through 2014. *Review of Educational Research, 84*(4), 1151–1191.

Kristoff, N. (2014, February 23). When even the starting line is out of reach. *New York Times.* Retrieved from http://www.nytimes.com.

Lilly, J., & Todd, R. (2015, May 22). W. Va. mine wars, redneck folklore, and more. *Inside Appalachia* [Audio podcast]. Retrieved from http://wvpublic.org.

Lowenstein, K. L. (2009). The work of multicultural teacher education: Reconceptualizing white teacher candidates as learners. *Review of Educational Research, 79*(1), 163–196.

MacDonald, E., & Shirley, D. (2009). *The mindful teacher*. New York: Teachers College Press.

Miller Dressler, M. (1973). Appalachia. *West Virginia Encyclopedia*. Retrieved from http://www.wvencyclopedia.org.

National Center for Educational Statistics (NCES). (2013). *The condition of education 2013*. Washington, DC: U.S. Department of Education.

Pollard, K. M. (2004). A "new diversity": Race and ethnicity in the Appalachian region. Washington, DC: Population Reference Bureau and Appalachian Regional Commission. Retrieved from http://www.prb.org.

Utt, J., & Tochluck, S. (2016). White teacher, know thyself: Improving anti-racist praxis through racial identity development. *Urban Education*. Retrieved from http://journals.sagepub.com.

Zajonc, A. (2009). *Meditation as contemplative inquiry*. Great Barrington, MA: Lindisfarne.

Chapter Five

Deep Listening, Authentic Dialogue

Supporting the Work of Critical Global Education

Tami Augustine, Ohio State University, Columbus, Ohio

In the current educational environment, teacher education programs are preparing candidates to contend with "the pressure to teach to the test and the narrowing and scripting of curriculum" (Kumashiro, 2009, p. xxvi). Faced with such challenges, it remains important that teacher educators create space to think critically about the world and utilize contemplative practices that can support this endeavor. It is at this intersection of policy, curriculum, and teacher education that this chapter on contemplative practices intervenes to offer foundational tools to develop skills needed to engage in the work of critical global education.

This chapter discusses research-based findings that focus on the ways preservice teachers defined deep listening and authentic dialogue, as well as successful classroom practices that developed their ability to practice deep listening and authentic dialogue. There is clear alignment of the skills and dispositions critical global education seeks to develop and what contemplative practices offer: openness to new information/open-mindedness, awareness of more than one perspective/perspective consciousness, development of critical-thinking skills, and understanding of interconnectedness and multiple perspectives (Kahane, 2009; Sable, 2014).

CRITICAL GLOBAL EDUCATION AND
CONTEMPLATIVE PRACTICE

Open-mindedness and a sense of connection to humanity in preservice teachers are foundational skills when implementing classroom practice that seeks to disrupt dominant hegemonic narratives. Integrating critical global education and contemplative practice with preservice teachers supports dialogic classroom spaces that disrupts what qualifies as truth. Critical global education (CGE) critiques Eurocentric versions of history to encompass multiplicities related to gender, race, ethnicity, language, religion, history, and culture. Through the examination of issues of power and oppression, issues of equity and diversity maintain a central place in the global education framework.

Critical global education consists of multiple components. Most important for this study is the inclusion of critical global perspectives and reflexivity to avoid appropriating "global cultures, histories, and experiences to further claim the superiority of specific national/cultural ways of being" (Subedi, 2010, p. 2). This is a critical link between CGE and contemplative practice. Supported by contemplative practice, deep listening and authentic dialogue becomes possible through the use of reflexivity and simultaneously creates space for such reflexivity. In this sense, what is often experienced in classrooms as listening and dialogue are transformed to become both a result of and an aspect of contemplative practice.

For the purposes of this study, contemplative practices are defined as assisting in the creation of new categories, openness to new information, and an implicit awareness of more than one perspective (Barbezat & Bush, 2014; Palmer & Zajonc, 2010). Examples of contemplative practice include sitting, walking, and lying-down meditation; embracing stillness and silence; reflection and questioning; guided imagery; freewriting; and the creation of visual images.

Contemplative practices are an "invitation to explore students' own beliefs and views so that the first-person, critical inquiry becomes an investigation rather than an imposition of particular views" (Barbezat & Bush, 2014, p. 23). By implementing contemplative practices, educators make a conscious choice to encourage students to sit with the tension that comes from seeking to understand new perspectives.

METHODOLOGY

As part of a larger research project, the rationale for this study was to examine the role of integrating contemplative practices into a methods course for preservice teachers that utilized a CGE framework. Questions that guided this research are as follows: (1) How does teaching a methods course using contemplative pedagogy contribute to the development of the habits of mind in global education? and (2) How does teaching a methods course using contemplative pedagogy advance how educators teach from a globally minded perspective? Participants included seven female and three male pre-service teachers, ranging from twenty-one to twenty-three years old. The semester-long course was taught as part of a Middle Childhood Education licensure program.

Data collected from participants' course work, reflections, group discussion, recordings of class sessions, and four individual interviews with each participant were analyzed in a sequential manner, examined for developing themes and patterns, and reflected upon to ensure the greatest accuracy (Hatch, 2002). Most relevant to this chapter was the emergence of "deep listening" and "authentic dialogue" as major themes in the data. Open-ended interview questions focused on developing definitions of these terms and understanding preservice teacher experiences with listening and dialogue, to gather thick descriptions that are a hallmark of qualitative data collection (Lincoln & Guba, 1985).

Utilizing open coding through the analysis process permitted the representation of individual and classroom community perspectives in each category (Strauss & Corbin, 1998). Data within and across class sessions were categorized and analyzed and then reorganized into categories. Informed by this data analysis, the remainder of this chapter will discuss the ways preservice teachers defined deep listening and authentic dialogue, and it provides classroom practices preservice teachers identified as successful in developing their ability to practice deep listening and authentic dialogue to foster the dispositions needed to engage in the work of CGE.

METHODS COURSE

The methods course[1] discussed in this chapter placed "struggling with ambiguity" at the center of learning (Kumashiro, 2009). In order to honor the voices and experiences from around the world, curriculum included materials and perspectives that problematize Western-centric approaches to education that reinforce the hegemonic discourse too often evident in classrooms. Course readings included, but were not limited to, *Against Common Sense* (Kumashiro, 2009), "Listening to Strangers: Classroom Discussion in Democratic Education" (Parker, 2010), and "Decolonizing the Curriculum for Global Perspectives" (Subedi, 2013).

DEVELOPING DEEP LISTENING AND AUTHENTIC DIALOGUE

Embedded in the work of contemplative practice and CGE are opportunities for interaction and dialogue. Dialogue in this sense is conceptualized as the process that creates "the truth between us," challenges unquestioned realities, and is "humanizing speech that challenges and resists domination" (Dillard, 2006, p. 22). Creating successful dialogue in educative settings takes into account speaking in terms people understand based on lived experience. Simply providing space for conversations is not enough to encourage authentic dialogue. Participants must be willing, relationships must be committed, and agendas must reflect the voice of the oppressed instead of the oppressor.

Patricia Williams (1997) describes the process and aims of authentic dialogue as "creating a community [engaged in] this most difficult work of negotiating real divisions, of considering boundaries before we go crashing through, and of pondering our differences before we can ever agree on the terms of our sameness" (p. 4). This type of dialogue reflects the complexity and fluidity of power and knowledge.

Using contemplative pedagogy to support deep listening and authentic dialogue was essential to the success of classroom interactions that permitted preservice teachers to engage with material that expanded their understanding of the world and to shift away from Eurocentric interpretations of global issues. The remainder of this section will highlight the instructional strategies preservice teachers identified as central to developing deep listening and authentic dialogue and increased their understanding of global perspectives.

Classroom Environment

Cynthia Dillard (2006) states that classroom spaces should be open, hospitable, balance the individual and the community, encourage dialogue, and give opportunities for reflection. To achieve these goals, arrangement of the classroom space included the following: desks were arranged in small groups to support student-to-student interaction, quiet music played as students entered the room, and coffee and tea was brewed with students often bringing food to share. The Special Place of Tranquility (SPOT) occupied the front of the room (Bright Dawn, 2016).

The SPOT was a place where preservice teachers could leave items that distracted from learning or things they wanted to celebrate. As Amy[2] explained, "I enjoy having a safe space to place objects that are important to us or are stressors. . . . I put my planner there because I am constantly thinking about what I need to get done. By putting my planner up there, I could focus on the discussion in class, rather than being distracted by seeing my planner right at my seat with me." Preservice teachers shared quotes they felt applied to course work, pictures, student work, and even a cough drop in hopes of leaving one's cough at the door.

Each class concluded with Connecting with Stillness, a three- to five-minute period to pause and slow down. Students were given choices such as drawing, writing, meditating, watching videos that focused on slowing down, and watching instructor-created videos. Sasha summed up Connecting with Stillness as follows: "We see the positive images and music. It's just . . . inspirational quotes, reading that set the tone for the way you live the rest of the day or a week. It just sticks with you." Often the focus of education lies on the external. Making the inward focus of Connecting with Stillness a priority helped preservice teachers make meaning from their learning and integrate new information and perspectives (Immordino-Yang, Christodou-lou, & Singh, 2012).

Mindfulness

While data revealed that contemplative practices had a positive impact on laying the groundwork for work in CGE, preservice teachers reported through online discussions and interviews that mindfulness meditation was most impactful. Mindfulness meditation was defined as "the awareness that emerges through paying attention on purpose, in the present moment, and nonjudgmentally to the unfurling experience moment to moment" (Kabat-Zinn, 2003, p. 144). Chosen for its straightforward and secular introduction to meditation, a video was shown that introduced the practice as a way to take a moment to calm and regain focus for the day (Boroson, 2016).

Responses from preservice teachers reflected two themes in their percep-tions: (1) meditation as a way to slow down and reflect in a fast-moving society and (2) meditation as a way to prepare oneself for learning. Accord-ing to Thomas, "I think it's like mentally you can say, 'Okay. This is our time now. We're not just going to start right away.' I can reflect or relax before having to think really hard and engage in these types of conversa-tions."

Amy summarized the positive influence of meditation for the large major-ity of preservice teachers in this study:

> I love doing the minute meditation, because I come into class, and a million things on my mind and then I'm like, okay gotta start class, gotta talk about readings, and then we do our meditation. And then I'm like, oooh . . . and it sets you up to really learn in a good way. Not just get through this get through this . . . you don't feel like you're getting through it anymore. You feel like you're actually learning in an open kind of way.

Like Amy, Bo used the meditation to focus. "The meditation part for me . . . I think it lets me get in the moment and prepare myself for this. . . . Let's just worry about this for right now. It helps me to be a lot more present." Contemplative practices readied preservice teachers to develop knowledge, skills, and dispositions to critically examine materials for particular worldviews and grapple with complex global issues. Including contemplative practices provided preservice teachers with skills needed to navigate difficult topics that challenged their worldview in an open-minded and dialogic manner.

Instructional Strategies

Strategies described in this section are informed by Walter Parker's (2010) work on creating classroom discussion for democratic education, Thich Nhat Hanh's (2013) work on compassionate listening, and Katherine Shultz's (2003) work on locating listening at the center of teaching and learning. Using this work, each class discussion focused on (1) reciprocity—privileging what the speaker says from their perspective and setting aside any reaction; (2) humility—acknowledging the speakers' expertise of their experience and that the listener's knowledge is incomplete; and (3) caution—responding with care by carefully considering what is added to the dialogue.

Talking Chips

Talking Chips is a small-group strategy designed to promote equal participation by each member of the group. Each group member receives two chips, and each time a group member wishes to speak, they place a chip on the table. When one person is finished speaking, another person places the chip on the table to continue the dialogue. Participants may not add to the dialogue a second time until each member of the group has shared.

In order to critically examine global topics, each student discussed the assigned topic from the perspective of a particular nation—each from a different region of the world. For Emma this strategy helped her consider another's motives behind their stance: "I usually kind of listen, I don't really let it sink in and consider it enough to change my opinions. But now I had to listen and consider where the other leaders were coming from and why. This made me stop and consider—are my needs actually more important?" When coupled with deep listening, Talking Chips increased comfort with wait time as it created pauses in the dialogue. Waiting for the speakers to complete their thought, contributing a chip in order to speak, and not being able to speak a second time until everyone else had contributed eliminated interruptions and helped lessen the listener's need to respond, thereby increasing the ability to listen and respond with reciprocity, humility, and caution.

Think—Pair—Listen

Working in pairs across multiple class sessions, three exercises were implemented using the following topics to guide the exercise: (1) tell a personally meaningful story; (2) discuss two conflicting global perspectives discussed in class; and (3) take two different perspectives on a "controversial" issue discussed in class. Each pair went through the steps below with each exercise, each person taking time to speak and listen:

- The listener listened for understanding, the emotion behind the story, and what was not shared.
- The listener reflected back what the speaker shared through restating, without adding to or interpreting the story.
- The speaker listened to establish if the listener's reflection captured the most important aspects of the story and clarified any points missed.
- After both partners shared and each felt there was clear understanding, the partners continued their dialogue.

For Amy, the Think—Pair—Listen activity signified a shift in her listening skills. "I am respectful and listen. But what I've discovered is that I don't actually really listen and reconsider what I am thinking and believing. When I had to listen to a conflicting perspective and I had to repeat back what they said without commenting or disagreeing . . . especially when we did the controversial issues, I had to actually really listen."

Preservice teachers stated these exercises challenged them because they (1) wanted to interrupt to share a story they felt was a similar experience or to disagree on a particular point; (2) felt unprepared to reflect back what their partner had shared without taking notes; and (3) felt uncomfortable correcting their partner if what they reflected back was not accurate.

Recordings of these three class sessions revealed longer pauses between comments in conjunction with comments that reflected greater depth of understanding of topics and concepts. Through in-class written reflections and online discussion following these practices, preservice teachers made similar observations by commenting that honoring another's perspective became easier as they no longer felt compelled to share their perspective, and they became more comfortable with the silence created in the space between the dialogue.

Serial Testimony

All preservice teachers in this study identified Serial Testimony as the most advanced and challenging listening strategy. Serial Testimony creates dialogue that embeds space for silence, privileges the speakers and their perspectives, and asks the listeners to seek to understand rather than respond. It invites each person's voice and reflections into the classroom space.

The instructor initiates the activity with a guiding question. One class session where this strategy was implemented focused on global citizenship, which was framed by course readings and President Obama's speech on the use of chemical weapons in Syria and potential U.S. intervention. The guiding question was, Who is a global citizen?[3]

- Each student writes his or her reflection on the guiding question prior to beginning, to allow greater focus on listening and not on what the student might share.
- In groups no larger than ten, one person volunteers to begin the dialogue and then each person shares around the circle one at a time.
- Expectations are as follows: (1) students take time to write down what they will share in the circle; (2) students go in order around the circle; (3) there are no interruptions or cross-talking; (4) students may share only what they initially reflected upon in response to the guiding question and may not respond to what others have shared (emphasizing sharing one's perspective on the class material); (5) no notes are taken; and (6) students listen in silence.
- This strategy was implemented in multiple class sessions, and with each subsequent use of the strategy the next step differed to continue to expand the deep listening and authentic dialogue practice. The order of next steps is as follows: (1) the process is repeated, and students share their experiences about the strategy; (2) session students repeat the process, responding to points that others have made; (3) a new guiding question is posed by the instructor based on information shared; and (4) based on the themes discussed, the class breaks into smaller groups to continue dialogue around a chosen theme.

There are two areas for consideration that were not part of the initial expectations. There was no time limit on how long students could share. This may be an important addition depending on the topic and group of students. While not directed to do so, when one person finished speaking, the next paused for a few seconds to be sure the person finished sharing. They did not ask each other, "Are you finished?" but allowed the silence to dictate when one person was finished and the next should continue. This created silence and space between the dialogue that permitted students to reflect further.

During a group interview, the preservice teachers came to consensus that each of these strategies (Talking Chips, Think—Pair—Listen, and Serial Testimony) shifted how they thought about and practiced deep listening. The Serial Testimony signaled the greatest shift in their deep listening practice. Elton commented,

I like the quote[4] where it talked about the first thing you need to do in a dialogue is not to speak. Then open your mind and remain calm. And I like that because I feel like sometimes I get passionate in my responses which leads me to jump in. So I need to just sit back and put myself in the speaker's shoes and just listen. Then I can sit in the space between and think about what I want to add.

Each strategy asked preservice teachers to listen and speak with reciprocity, humility, and caution. Each strategy provided the scaffolding and support to enable preservice teachers to develop skills needed to engage with materials and dialogue that disrupted American narratives and perspectives about global issues.

EXPERIENCES IN CLASSROOM DIALOGUE

Engaging in Deep Listening

Early in this study, preservice teachers identified deep listening and authentic dialogue as playing a prominent role in developing the dispositions necessary to engage in the work of CGE. After course readings and classroom experiences, preservice teachers described deep listening as a slower and more thoughtful interaction. Deep listening included honoring and considering another's perspective with care. Critical global education encourages the practice of including global perspectives that honor cultural practices and knowledges of people around the world. Practicing deep listening assisted in balancing the power dynamics.

For Sophie, deep listening meant being open-minded and listening without formulating a response or judgment: "A lot of deep listening is understanding how someone feels about something. Being able to gauge their emotions and attitudes toward whatever they're talking about. And being open minded because if you're not, you're not listening to what the other person is saying and you are preparing your rebuttals as they're talking." Aligning with Parker's (2010) discussion of the importance of removing the aggression of the listener, Amy echoed Sophie's understanding of deep listening: "I have a problem with really listening. I can listen to people, but I just want to respond. So I think deep listening is just closing down your own thoughts and hearing what someone else has to say."

Deep listening asked that preservice teachers, according to Jennifer, "pause and fully acknowledge that someone has something important to say and to think about it before you respond and to show that you value it." Deep listening also created the ability to have what preservice teachers would come to call authentic dialogue and laid the groundwork for them to disagree with one another as part of an interconnected learning community.

Engaging in Authentic Dialogue

Preservice teachers defined authentic dialogue as dialogue where deep listening was required in order to thoughtfully and respectfully challenge each other's views while still honoring another's perspective. When asked about authentic dialogue, Sophie stated, "Authentic dialogue you have to listen, not to respond, but listen deeply and then thoughtfully respond if that is what is appropriate. You might even just be quiet for a while." Bo expanded on this: "It's hard in today's society . . . it's hard to sit down and have a conversation. But I think deep listening—sitting there, letting the person get out what they want to say first and then you can respond with authenticity."

Another common theme for preservice teachers was the role authentic dialogue played in practicing open-mindedness and being able to consider global perspectives that shift the dialogue away from Eurocentric narratives. Emma emphasized this when stating, "In order for it to be an actual authentic dialogue you have to be willing to listen deeply and you have to actually want to hear the new information or perspectives. If you are closed off and you don't want to hear that information you're not going to have a real dialogue with them." Elton echoed this connection between deep listening and authentic dialogue: "When you're listening . . . not just in one ear and out the other . . . but like our deep listening. Relating and understanding what's actually being said, comprehending it. Understanding it from their perspective, then bring in another perspective when you exchange ideas." For preservice teachers to experience authentic dialogue about multiple and conflicting perspectives foundational to CGE, preservice teachers identified deep listening is an essential ingredient.

CONCLUSION

The findings in this chapter suggest that using instructional strategies focused on the contemplative practices of deep listening and authentic dialogue developed the dispositions necessary for preservice teachers to become more critically minded and to be more open to multiple and conflicting perspectives. Pam captured the overall experiences of the preservice teachers when she stated, "I guess all this—just instead of looking at someone and thinking, 'You're wrong,' listening to that and responding, 'Why do you believe that? What makes you think that? Make me understand what's in your head,' instead of being like, 'No, that's completely off base because it's not what I think or that's not what is best for me.'" Throughout this study, preservice teachers discussed the connection of deep listening and authentic dialogue to developing the skills embedded within CGE. Most preservice teachers began the study wanting to avoid complex issues in the classroom because they were afraid of losing control, feared student arguments, or were unsure of how to create a dialogic space. Practicing deep listening and authentic dialogue assisted them in being able to work through some of their fears so they felt more prepared to have such conversations. As Amy explained,

> I think it's helping. I sat down with my mom and my dad and my mom is so Catholic and I was like, "You know what, what if you're wrong? What if somebody else is right?" And we have this big conversation and it was great. . . . I'm more comfortable having these conversations with people that I thought I would never challenge their view. It's good because if I can have that conversation with my mom, I could have that conversation with my students.

This study puts forth that in order to equip teacher candidates with the ability to address CGE curriculum that problematizes the American and Western-centric approaches to education, this must be modeled in the teacher education classroom.

Preservice teachers emphasized that they are only as open-minded as experiences and knowledge gained demand them to be. Examining whose voice is present and whose is missing in assignments, examining issues of power, and critiquing information for not only what is said but also how it is said became a transformative aspect of the methods course that would not have been as impactful without deep listening and authentic dialogue practice.

Bo's statement summarizes the challenges preservice teachers faced:

> Just from hearing from so many different perspectives, and seeing how we all are interconnected, and intertwined in some way, and what you do does have an impact on another person whether you believe it or not. You always want to think you're that way [open-minded], but until you actually grapple with this type of work that we've been doing, I think then, you really figure out that you are or are not. I mean are you really willing to be challenged like that?

This study speaks to the importance of (1) providing necessary tools for preservice teachers to continue critiquing hegemonic systems and remain open to different ways of thinking and being; and (2) integrating strategies that support deep listening and authentic dialogue as a foundation to becoming more critically minded. Education that encourages inner and intellectual work challenges preservice teachers to examine how they view the world and their place in, and responsibility to, the larger global community.

ESSENTIAL IDEAS TO CONSIDER

- Contemplative practices can assist in developing the skill sets needed to become more open and globally minded.

- When supported by contemplative practice, what is often experienced in classrooms as listening and dialogue are transformed to become deep listening and authentic dialogue and are a result of and an aspect of contemplative practice.
- Using instructional strategies focused on the contemplative practices of deep listening and authentic dialogue supported the development of the dispositions necessary for preservice teachers to become more critically minded and to be more open to multiple and conflicting perspectives.
- Deep listening and authentic dialogue differ from listening and dialogue that is the norm in most classrooms. Such skills must be intentionally cultivated through scaffolding instructional strategies intended for such purpose.

NOTES

1. Course goals and objectives can be found in the appendix.
2. All names are pseudonyms.
3. This question led to a discussion of issues of power in relation to global citizenship. Critical examination of who has and who is denied that access is central to the CGE framework.
4. When asked what he would say to Osama Bin Laden after 9/11, Thich Nhat Hanh stated, "The first thing I would do is listen. I would try to understand why he had acted in that cruel way. I would try and understand all of the suffering that had led him to violence. It might not be easy to listen in that way, I would have to remain calm and lucid" (as cited in Parker, 2010, p. 2828).

REFERENCES

Barbezat, D. P., & Bush, M. (2014). *Contemplative practices in higher education: Powerful methods to transform teaching and learning.* San Francisco: Jossey-Bass.
Boroson, Martin. (2016). One moment meditation. One Moment Company. Retrieved May 7, 2016, from http://www.onemomentmeditation.com.
Bright Dawn. (2016). Special place of tranquility (SPOT). Institute for American Buddhism. Retrieved May 7, 2016, from http://www.brightdawn.org.
Dillard, C. B. (2006). *On spiritual strivings: Transforming an African American woman's academic life.* Albany, NY: SUNY.
Hanh, T. N. (2013). *The art of communicating.* New York: HarperCollins.
Hatch, J. A. (2002). *Doing qualitative research in education settings.* Albany, NY: State University of New York Press.
Immordino-Yang, M. H., Christodoulou, J., & Singh, V. (2012). Rest is not idleness: Implications of the brain's default mode for human development and education. *Perspectives on Psychological Science, 7*, 352–364.
Kabat-Zinn, J. (2003). Mindfulness-based intervention in context: Past, present, and future. *Clinical Psychology Science and Practice, 10*(2), 144–156.
Kahane, D. (2009). Learning about obligation, compassion, and global justice: The places of contemplative pedagogy. *New Directions for Teaching and Learning, 118*, 49–60.
Kumashiro, K. K. (2009). *Against common sense: Teaching and learning toward social justice.* New York: Routledge.
Lincoln, Y. S., & Guba, E. G. (1985). *Naturalistic inquiry.* Beverly Hills, CA: Sage.
Palmer, P., & Zajonc, A. (2010). *The heart of higher education.* San Francisco: Jossey-Bass.

Parker, W. (2010). Listening to strangers: Classroom discussion in democratic education. *Teachers College Record, 112*(11), 2815–2832.

Sable, D. (2014). The unexpected consequences of applying mindfulness to critical thinking. Paper presented at the 2014 AAU Teaching Showcase, Sydney, New South Wales, Australia.

Shultz, K. (2003). *Listening: A framework for teaching across difference.* New York: Teachers College Press.

Strauss, A., & Corbin, J. (1998). *Basics of qualitative research: Techniques and procedures for developing grounded theory.* Thousand Oaks, CA: Sage.

Subedi, B. (Ed.). (2010). *Critical global perspectives: Rethinking knowledge about global societies.* Charlotte, NC: Information Age.

Subedi, B. (2013). Decolonizing the curriculum for global perspectives. *Educational Theory, 63*(6), 621–638.

Williams, P. J. (1997). *Seeing a colour-blind future: The paradox of race.* London: Virago.

Chapter Six

Toward Persistence

Contemplative Practices in Community College Teacher Education Programs

Heather Bandeen, Hamline University, Saint Paul, Minnesota

Contemplative practices support community college students by generatively shaping their "intellect, emotions and spirit" (Mackler, Aguilar, & Serena, 2008, p. 1). Defined broadly as "moment-by-moment" attentiveness, contemplative practices underscore nuanced meanings within a career that is characterized by wide-ranging curricular delivery and unrelentingly interpersonal interactions (Haynes, 2005, p. 2). On a community college campus where students may face multiple challenges when compared with university peers, student transitions to new roles as teaching professionals can be fraught with daunting complexity.

These challenges include remedial academic needs and language barriers as well as food and housing insecurity (CCSSE, 2005; Logue, 2015). At the same time, teacher education courses often tend to follow rote pragmatisms of "dos" and "don'ts" that can ignore the importance of equipping students with competencies to persist. When faculty members attend to "moments" of teaching in these early days, it can make all the difference. The importance of reshaping spaces where students learn to teach, as contemplative environments that attend to the whole person, cannot be overstated, particularly for those who feel disconnected and alone (Cozolino, 2013).

Contemplative practices can provide unique support for community college students while also offering universal pedagogical models that benefit all preservice teacher candidates. Research shows that contemplative work and practices of compassion can bolster student recovery after exposure to the "fearful stimuli" associated with major life disruptions and even daily disappointments (Mowe, 2015). There is much to be gained from pedagogical design that aims for a deeper understanding of the moment-by-moment work of teaching and learning. This design lends a framework to this chapter to address

1. volunteering, with emphasis on language and relational interconnectivity;
2. space, to mindfully shape teaching and learning within functional environments; and
3. reflection, by engaging with dimensions of growth and persistence.

This chapter will first briefly delve into unique challenges of two-year campuses and then outline a series of concrete strategies designed to support student persistence toward roles as thoughtful advocates for themselves and others, including community college peers and P–12 students.

Throughout the pedagogical integration of contemplative practices and course design, the faculty must remain mindful of programmatic connections to four-year institutions. The ultimate goal is that these holistic efforts will attend to students' "intellect, emotions and spirit" while also planning for graduation and licensure requirements (Mackler, Aguilar, & Serena, 2008, p. 1).

THE COMMUNITY COLLEGE CAMPUS

Though community colleges do not typically license teachers, students frequently complete their general education requirements and early teacher education course work on two-year campuses. In fact, the nation's 1,123 community colleges serve nearly half of all U.S. students (American Association of Community Colleges, 2015). Two-year campuses attract numerous first-generation college students, and many receive Pell Grant funding (Mullin, 2012). In my former faculty role at a Minnesota community college, students ranged in age from sixteen to sixty-five and represented wide-ranging academic abilities.

Among the numerous postsecondary options available today, community colleges provide affordable, flexible course pathways that allow students to work and balance obligations close to home. It is common for community colleges to offer an array of program delivery choices that include online, hybrid, evening, and condensed weekend formats. This means that, while individual courses may be readily available, students do not have consistent opportunities for on-campus relationships and in-person support, typically offered on traditional, residential campuses.

Additionally, most two-year campuses are open access. This means that grade point averages, prerequisites, and standardized test scores are not barriers to admission and, at the same time, may lead to student enrollment in teacher education courses while simultaneously completing remedial, noncredit mathematics, reading, or writing courses. This is often in stark contrast to university teacher education programs that require students to meet criteria for program admission and then complete a series of sequential benchmarks with support from peer and faculty relationships.

The hidden disadvantage to programmatic flexibility is that community college students can feel adrift without the structure of traditional teacher education programs and, oftentimes, lose sight of their "end game"—successful graduation and eventual employment. For example, the absence of formalized out-of-class support systems can be problematic (e.g., cohort peers, residence hall roommates, and faculty advisors). Such relationships often provide the keys to propelling students toward completing course work while also bolstering deeper understandings of themselves as they relate to others (Bellafante, 2014).

In fact, community college students are more likely than their university peers to face four or more unpredictable variables, such as part-time attendance, thirty-hour workweeks, and single parenthood, that can further contribute to isolation and sidetrack academic focus (CCSSE, 2005). This can mean that students, particularly those who are overloaded by such variables, may operate in "survival mode" and eschew important attentiveness to meaningful relationships and tasks that inevitably support degree completion.

CONTEMPLATIVE PRACTICES: CONCRETE STRATEGIES FOR THE CLASSROOM

In early teacher education courses, community college students are first introduced to the monumental transition to roles as new teachers. When students can be guided toward recognizing and grasping at the relational touch points that accompany this shift, such as buoying friendships, inner strength, and peaceful environments, they can avoid perseverating on the inevitable failures that will happen along the way (Mowe, 2015). In the sections below, a series of concrete strategies, shaped by elements of volunteering, spaces, and reflection, are offered to support students' self-awareness during the transition to becoming teachers—along the continuum of "intellect, emotions and spirit" (Mackler, Aguilar, & Serena, 2008, p. 1).

Volunteering

First and foremost, students need substantive opportunities beyond the two-year campus to engage with teachers, P–12 students, and community members. When these opportunities are crafted by the faculty as intentionally immersive and relational, students can be guided toward attunement with the smallest details of early encounters with others.

Immersive Requirements

Teacher education courses at community colleges should routinely require approximately fifty clinical placement hours to immerse students in school environments with a focus on engaged community membership. Frequently, as a contrast, students typically have minimal classroom field study hour requirements in their first courses. Extended immersion can lend itself to "a kind of deep knowing" that is most beneficial (Plante, 2010, p. 240); it allows students to experience the daily joys and difficulties inherent to a teaching role.

Students gain opportunities to observe not only teacher-to-student interactions but also the teacher-to-teacher interactions—the typically unseen activity during a given workday. The goal is that students begin to envision themselves as members of an educational community rather than as mere bystanders who visit occasionally. As a contrast to more passive, superficial interactions with teachers and P–12 students, this intentional, sustained work can provide the impetus for a deepening understanding—over time—of the underlying complexities that are linked to this career pathway and life commitment.

Community college students can be pedagogically directed toward becoming intentional about how they engage with others and record notes to account for the nuanced, daily mix of moment-by-moment exchanges of language and action. When students attend to the smallest details with this focus, they begin to understand how words and actions ripple into the shaping of a learning environment where each contribution can be recognized and valued. During these early experiences, students can be encouraged to practice compassionate advocacy skills via careful language use and supportive, reciprocal actions.

Specifically, students can be asked to shadow teachers to better understand the implicit job demands and record observed methods of coping. Students can be guided toward recognizing the need for carving out time for themselves, as future teachers, with strategies such as silence, deep breathing, journaling, and interpersonal distance as appropriate. Such discussions can cultivate curiosity regarding ways that current teachers can support one another with language, environmental design, and time allocation.

Introspective Examination of Community Contexts

Before students begin volunteering, they must become familiar with the surrounding community and better understand that teaching and learning processes do not only occur within sterile, bounded spaces. They happen everywhere. The goal is to help students attend to strategies for maintaining their own emergent professional and personal balance as they encounter a barrage of information within these new environments.

Such attentiveness to influences beyond the school building can allow community college students to delve into complex factors that shape the patterns of P–12 student and teacher interactions that ultimately occur inside of classrooms (Haynes, 2005, p. 5). For example, what signals and language denote the value of families and community? From moment to moment, how does the experience of riding a bus and walking on a sidewalk influence impressions of community membership? What are the rituals of transitioning across contexts as community members interact (e.g., buying groceries and walking children to school)? Who is included and excluded? What becomes privileged and what is not? What is immediately noticeable and what becomes evident over time?

During course discussions, these questions can be extended to reflect upon the habitual tendencies of students' own interpersonal reactivity. The biases that each of us hold can ultimately influence what we recognize and gravitate toward in a school environment. Some pedagogical questions to consider include the following: How do community college students personally feel in response to language that is used to welcome others? What are their perceptions regarding space (or lack thereof) allocated for gathering or introspection? What activities do they think could be made available to cultivate balanced lives?

Relational Service Pilgrimages

Teacher education courses can also be designed with relational group pilgrimages to analyze ways that their identities palpably shift among learning contexts. There are distinct benefits to leaving campus together to travel to another place for learning. When students complete volunteer hours collectively in this way, they ultimately gain more time for focused reflection. To achieve this, group transportation can be arranged to and from other environments, such as temporary housing centers, food pantries, and after-school programs. The concept of a "pilgrimage" can underscore the sanctity of shared spaces that provide basics for life, such as food and shelter.

Such a pilgrimage, when designed as a shared experience among new teachers, allows students to practice what it means to transition into and also from life experiences. It can be a delicate dance to honor intense interpersonal experiences while also returning, whole, to attend one's own life. To underscore the attention to such transitions, shared transit times can allow for a discussion with sustained attention to multiple perspectives immediately afterward (e.g., What is difficult about leaving? What questions do you still have?). This is in notable contrast to passing time on digital devices that distract from—rather than enhance—an understanding of how particular moments have sparked new, profound understandings.

During travel together, students can be encouraged to engage in sustained quiet reflection or attentive consultation with peers where they intentionally focus on language use and silences. The goal is that students will carry this practice into other parts of their lives where mindful attention to processes such as eating, sleeping, and engaging with others will support a healthy mindset. By explicitly embedding tools of persistence within college-related experiences like these, students gain a familiarity with how it feels to employ healthy transitional coping skills that support well-being during times of change.

These immersive volunteer experiences profoundly shift student experiences in teacher education courses. The uptick in campus course participation cannot be overstated as students draw upon vivid moments with a sense of profound ownership. They also learn incrementally to monitor their own impulses and inclinations in chaotic environments. This is in contrast to the typical acquisition of prescriptive processes, as dogma, often found in career-oriented courses (Grace, 2011). Further, students gain an acute awareness of support networks for themselves as they embark on the growing, learning, and becoming process of what it means to be a teacher. These experiences are transformative in that respect as well.

Space

The creation of inclusive, safe spaces beyond the community college classroom becomes all the more important when students tend to encounter "non-academic barriers" that can inhibit persistence from moment to moment (CCRC, 2013, p. 1). As Daniel Barbezat and Allison Pingree (2012) explain, contemplative practices allow instructors to "endeavor to teach the whole person, with an intention to go beyond the mere transference of facts and theories" (p. 177). Because of this, teacher education pedagogy should be mindful of ways that informal time and environments can be leveraged to broaden student experiences each week and, ultimately, contribute to persistence.

Informal Time

Oftentimes before a typical community college class session, students can be found lingering in hallways without engaging with one another; instead, they tend to sit alone engrossed with digital devices. To expand reflective opportunities for students, one option is to open the doors early and even provide healthy snacks. The addition of food can add irreplaceable communal dynamics to reduce uncertainty in these transitional moments before class begins. Food can be used to signal a welcoming environment where it is acceptable to observe, share stories, and also listen in companionable silence. This practice reshapes the notion of the classroom as not a teacher-guided space with a scripted start and end time but rather a multiuse, shared location.

Over time, it is not uncommon that students begin arriving early to make connections and engage in ongoing, analytical "unpacking" of their learning. Students who volunteer at the same school can be overheard discussing patterned behaviors of a particular P–12 student or wondering aloud about a set of rules. The tenor of these discussions tend, increasingly, to focus on personal reflection and to open toward new relationships that in turn support students' holistic growth. Friendships, partnerships for other classes, or even swapped resources provide tools of persistence. These informal dialogues then feed in-class discussions as students examine their shared fragile vulnerabilities and acknowledge viewpoints with attuned compassion.

Communal Space

Classroom organization can emerge as paramount when contemplative practices attend to the generative development of competencies toward persistence. During teaching and learning, students benefit from space to connect with others or to choose stillness. In my experience, circular tables provide a better option when compared with traditional rows by balancing power to foster a sense of community. We also remained mindful of using nearby gathering places for short activities and at times even opted for space in the campus community garden so students could exercise the choice of retreating.

Such spatial practices can be paired with walks, as a group, to locations like the counseling center to normalize the pursuit of emotional well-being when assuming new personal or professional roles. In doing so, practices of self-care are emphasized. Along the way, quiet campus spaces are also highlighted to emphasize the value of taking moments for reflective time that eschews multitasking. The hope is that these explicit descriptions of the functionality of campus spaces will cultivate mindful advocacy in future learning environments.

Reflection

Reading, writing, and listening are commonplace on college campuses; the contemplative framing of such engagement encourages students to think deeply about ways that their identity intersects with layers of course content. Personal connections to text can further support the development of meaning over time while increasing persistence. One common teacher education assignment requires students to submit reflective analyses of their P–12 experiences. With an eye toward a contemplative pedagogical lens, the language and silences of such assignments should be emphasized and made explicit.

As a faculty member on a community college campus, I noted that numerous students tended to use assignments like these to process memories when teachers or family members labeled them as "not made for school." These narratives can be emotionally charged and define success as, what Ellen Langer (2014) calls, "a zero sum commodity" (p. 30). Student adherence to such binary distinctions, like good or bad, fortunate or unfortunate, and achievement or failure, repeatedly revealed beliefs that some individuals are successful and others in turn are not. These divisive generalizations miss the value of examining concepts such as resilience and persistence and provide useful foundation for contemplative work.

Oftentimes, these narratives illustrated a startling divergence from those of many traditional teacher education students, who tend to remember P–12 schools as places where, more often than not, they felt supported. To process negatively charged emotions, students can be guided to practice perspective-taking to strengthen their inner persistent voice. Such processing also supports students to consider strategies for responding to others, including breathing, language, and reflection.

Discussions and reflective writing can be designed to help students to gain "a broader and deeper sense of how their learning fits into the fabric of their lives" rather than how it may be measured by rigid metrics (Barbezat & Pingree, 2012, p. 186). In sum, students can be encouraged to define, for themselves, a framework of balance and success.

Personal Reflection Tied to Purpose

When students arrive to a two-year campus and enroll, they are often exploring the teaching profession for the first time. Most often, they have not yet declared a formal major. This means that students scrutinize, resist, and question facets of "the world of work" while considering what it might mean to select a lifelong career path. To support such exploration, time for contemplative reflection can help students to develop curiosity about themselves and others. This intentional "meaning making" can encompass all areas of their lives while spurring mindful development toward a future vocation, whether teaching is in their future or not (Barbezat & Pingree, 2012).

Taking time to process how activities that fill their lives do (or do not) emulate their interconnected needs can be powerful. For example, what does it mean to derive purpose from daily work? When it becomes apparent that the smallest interactions can be modified to better support a measured, healthy approach to commitments and relationships, students can learn to attend to moments with others—and alone—that support their persistence over time. Such reflection can take many forms and does not need to focus solely on teaching.

Private Journaling

Cultivating a routine of private journal writing can benefit students beyond the scope of any course and underscores a particular contemplative practice that Langer (2014) refers to as "mindfulness." Mindfulness signals an explicit focus away from goals to the process of monitoring our interconnected emotions, thoughts, and motivations to enhance and support moment-to-moment attentiveness. Students may ask, What is expected by others? What do I expect of myself? How do my seemingly insignificant choices align with my long-term well-being?

The physical act of writing on paper cultivates sustained focus on a stream of thoughts apart from iterative virtual interactions where short, often disjointed texts demand immediate feedback from others. When students are encouraged to reflect deeply about the automaticity of daily choices, they can begin to recognize how such decisions ultimately shape persistence within the nuances of their academic and life trajectory. Such automaticity can include frequent multitasking that characterizes day-to-day existence for students and often produces an absent-minded experience, such as not recalling details of driving when texting, talking, or eating.

Letter to Myself . . . in the Future

A variation on private journaling involves asking students to write letters to themselves that a faculty member can mail at a future time. This exercise extends reminders beyond the scope of a given class and helps students to become "comfortable with uncertainty" during this period of immense change in their lives (Haynes, 2005, p. 6). Students can learn to be attentive to their feelings, as shaped by context, and develop an increased sense of objectivity that stems from time and distance.

It also provides a tangible means for students to reflect on growth and express compassion for their past and future selves through gentle reminders to value balance from minute to minute, hour to hour, and day to day. An added twist includes using a virtual platform that delivers e-mails on a future date (e.g., Futureme.org). The power of reading heartfelt thoughts from oneself amidst the distracting stream of news and reminders that fill virtual screens can serve as a nudge toward maintaining mindfulness. Oftentimes, students include messages of self-care and reminders to remain attuned to "what is most important."

Introspective Writing and Drawing

Short freewriting, concept-mapping, and drawing opportunities allow students to pause and examine their own beliefs. These in-class assignments are characterized by silence for an established period of time and may support important sensemaking prior to discussions. Such intentional focus can provide critical building blocks for organized approaches to outlining complex thoughts, in preparation for professional decision making.

Students can be encouraged to learn via multidimensional narratives and curricular connections as opposed to the recording of rote definitions—often offered by a traditional lecture (Grace, 2011). The use of drawing, freewriting, and other creative approaches may also add inclusive, inviting dimensions to strictly academic exercises. When students are asked to maintain attention and focus on a particular concept with permission to imagine, they are supported toward drafting patterns and understandings of what it might mean to connect and persist in new ways.

CONCLUSION

Community college students often navigate more unpredictable variables when compared with university peers, and as a result, some admit to feeling overwhelmed and isolated as they begin their degree programs (Cozolino, 2013). This chapter briefly delved into the unique challenges of two-year campuses and then outlined a series of concrete strategies designed to support student persistence throughout teacher education course work. Such practices can encourage students to embrace a reflective appreciation for what they may uniquely bring to future classrooms while also highlighting contemplative processes that provide support across all aspects of life.

Teacher education courses need to be purposively crafted to include design that attends to the small details and complex interactions of the profession of teaching.

Community college classrooms would benefit from an emphasis on three primary elements: volunteering opportunities with immersive hour requirements that emphasize community membership; learning spaces that are designed with student choice and self-care in mind; and reflection activities that allow students to imagine how concepts of vocation are interconnected with life balance. With these emphases, students can be supported toward greater self-awareness and future action with the knowledge that attending to "moments" during a school day can change their lives—and those of their future students.

ESSENTIAL IDEAS TO CONSIDER

- Students, particularly on two-year campuses, navigate unpredictable variables outside of the classroom, so pedagogy that focuses on the "whole student" is essential for persistence and success.
- Teaching within contemplative environments must cultivate methods to help students and teachers learn to function within new spaces while also learning to transition to—and from—these spaces in healthy, attuned ways.
- The benefits of sustained silence can never be understated, particularly in our wired world of constant connectivity.
- Without "moment-to-moment" attentiveness in teaching—and in life—we often ignore the rich meaning that ultimately informs every aspect our learning and lifelong growth.

REFERENCES

American Association of Community Colleges (AACC). (2015). AACC's 2015 Fact Sheet. Retrieved from http://www.aacc.nche.edu/AboutCC/Documents/FactSheet2015.pdf.

Barbezat, D., & Pingree, A. (2012). Contemplative pedagogy: The special role of teaching and learning centers. In J. E. Groccia & L. Cruz (Eds.), *To improve the academy*, vol. 31 (pp. 177–191). San Francisco: Jossey-Bass.

Bellafante, G. (2014, October 3). Community college students face a very long road to graduation. *New York Times*. Retrieved from http://www.nytimes.com.

Community College Research Center (CCRC). (2013). What we know about nonacademic student supports. Teachers College, Columbia University. Retrieved from http://ccrc.tc.columbia.edu.

Community College Survey of Student Engagement (CCSSE). (2005). Engaging students, challenging the odds: 2005 findings. Retrieved from https://www.ccsse.org.

Cozolino, L. (2013, March 19). Nine things educators need to know about the brain. Greater Good: The Science of a Meaningful Life @ Berkeley. Retrieved from http://greatergood.berkeley.edu.

Grace, F. (2011). Learning as a path, not a goal: Contemplative pedagogy—Its principles and practices. *Teaching Theology and Religion, 14*(2), 99–124.

Haynes, D. (2005). Contemplative practices and education: Making peace in ourselves and in the world. Teachers College, Columbia University. Center for Contemplative Mind in Society. Retrieved from http://www.contemplativemind.org.

Langer, E. (2014). *Mindfulness*. Boston: Da Capo.

Logue, J. (2015, December). House and home: Study finds hundreds of students at 10 different community colleges reported homelessness, food insecurity or both. *Inside Higher Ed*. Retrieved from https://www.insidehighered.com.

Mackler, J., Aguilar, A. P., & Serena, K. C. (2005). What is contemplative education and what are some ways to introduce it into higher education in Mexico? University of Quintana Roo, Department of Language Education. Retrieved from http://www.contemplativemind.org.

Mowe, S. (2015). Resilience and the brain: An interview with Richard Davidson. Garrison Institute. Retrieved from https://www.garrisoninstitute.org.

Mullin, C. M. (2012, February). *Why access matters: The community college student body* (Policy Brief 2012-01PBL). Washington, DC: American Association of Community Colleges.

Plante, T. G. (Ed). (2010). *Contemplative practices in action: Spirituality, meditation, and health*. Westport, CT: Praeger/Greenwood.

Chapter Seven

Mindfulness and Student Teaching

Practice Makes Perfect (Just as You Are!)

Elizabeth G. Holtzman and Carolyn H. Obel-Omia, Rhode Island College, Providence, Rhode Island

Given the high level of demands and performance pressure during preservice teacher education, the need for self-care is essential. Preservice teachers experience many of the same challenges as beginning teachers in our current education culture of increasing accountability with decreasing resources. Mindfulness practice provides a path to engage fully in all that student teaching offers—to reflect on challenges and successes rather than on merely surviving. This chapter describes a cross-disciplinary collaboration supporting the introduction of mindfulness practice in an elementary education preservice teacher seminar.

STUDENT TEACHING STRESS

Student teaching is stressful. Preservice teachers stand with one foot in the college classroom as students and one foot in K–12 school classroom as teachers, with demands and expectations from both realms. As students, they are required to fulfill college requirements while subject to frequent teaching evaluations by supervisors. As preservice teachers, they experience many of the same challenges as beginning teachers, such as increasing demands of accountability with limited time and resources. Preservice teachers are also in the unique position of constantly being evaluated by cooperating teachers.

The stress induced by clinical teaching demands is a frequently noted phenomenon, due to common stressors such as limited time, student behavior, and heavy workload (Caires, Almeida, & Vieira, 2012; Gardner, 2010).

The stress can impact their newly developing teacher identity. Without coping strategies, teachers may react to challenging situations rather than developing thoughtful, reflective responses. In this cycle, teachers tend to experience fewer positive student interactions, leading to a sense of inefficacy as a teacher, which is inversely related to teacher burnout; as levels of efficacy decrease, the likelihood of burnout increases (Fives, Hamman, & Olivarez, 2007).

SUPPORTING PRESERVICE TEACHERS TO DEVELOP HEALTHY HABITS OF MIND

There are many ways to support preservice teachers in managing this stress. One increasingly used model focuses on developing dispositions or habits of mind to support teacher wellness (Weaver & Wilding, 2013). These include such skills as being attentive to multiple and diverse sources of data, reflective and nonjudgmental, flexible in problem solving, empathic, and resilient.

A viable way to develop such habits of mind is through mindfulness training (Roeser, Beers, Skinner, & Jennings, 2012). Several programs integrating mindfulness for teachers have emerged. These include modifying established programs such as Mindfulness-Based Stress Reduction for teachers (Flook, Goldberg, Pinger, Bonus, & Davidson, 2013), as well as specifically designed teacher social emotional learning and mindfulness programs, such as SMART (Roeser et al., 2013) and CARE (Jennings, Frank, Snowberg, Coccia, & Greenberg, 2013).

At the preservice level, the integration of contemplative practice with education courses is increasing. For example, Elizabeth Dorman (2015) uses mindfulness to support development of social emotional competencies in preservice teacher candidates. A course specifically for preservice teachers, Mindfulness-Based Wellness Education, has been found to increase health, self-efficacy, and mindfulness (Poulin, Mackenzie, Soloway, & Karayolas, 2008). While attractive, having a separate course is not always possible in time- and resource-limited teacher education programs.

Mindfulness can be defined many different ways. Robert Roeser, Ellen Skinner, Jeffry Beers, and Patricia Jennings (2012) define mindfulness as "a particular way of deploying attention and awareness in the present moment in a nonreactive and nonjudgmental manner that facilitates emotion regulation, stress reduction, and healthy social interactions" (p. 168). In addition to reducing stress and increasing choiceful reactions, mindfulness practices have also been shown to increase self-compassion (Frank, Reibel, Broderick, Cantrell, & Metz, 2013).

A preservice teaching seminar offers a natural community of shared experience and structure for collegial support. However, reflecting mainly on areas of need and challenge can attenuate a negative or complaining pattern of thinking and interacting. Indeed, there is a neurological tendency to spend more time and focus on negative or potentially harmful things than on positive or helpful ones (Hanson, 2013). This has been called the negativity bias (Rozin & Royzman, 2001).

Self-judgment is a habitual response for many students, which can lead to feelings of disengagement or stress. Mindfulness has been found to reduce the negativity bias (Kiken & Shook, 2011). Specifically, a facet of mindfulness that supports engagement and well-being is the ability to step back from automatic or habitual responses (Malinowski & Lim, 2015).

Mindfulness cultivates an observer-participant stance toward reality, which helps frame experiences as an ongoing process rather than an unchanging or fixed reflection of self. Additionally, mindfulness practice increases the capacity to experience intense emotion without being overwhelmed by it, creating space to support full engagement without the automatic negative or judgmental stance.

MINDFULNESS WITHIN A PRESERVICE TEACHER SEMINAR

This project was a collaboration between two professors of education, one in the elementary education (ELED) department and one in the counseling, educational leadership, and school psychology (CEP) department, at a college of education in a Northeastern city in the United States. The idea grew from the ELED professor's concern that preservice teachers were reporting high levels of stress and limited coping strategies. After seeing a presentation by the CEP professor on her work integrating mindfulness into elementary schools and the need for teacher wellness support, the ELED professor suggested a collaboration embedding mindfulness practice into her student teaching seminar.

Together, they invited a class of eight preservice teacher candidates to increase their self-care by developing a beginning mindfulness practice. All chose to participate. Written and oral discussion prompts provided the preservice teachers with ongoing opportunities to reflect on experiences in their classrooms through the lens of mindfulness and with self-compassion. Preservice teachers also participated in a daily gratitude exercise, recording what went well at the end of each teaching day to encourage the practice of acknowledging and giving time to reflect on their daily successes.

Mindfulness was introduced and taught during the first twenty minutes of six biweekly seminar sessions. Each session began with a brief shared practice to build community and support a present-centered, compassionate space for the preservice teachers as they transitioned from the elementary school day to the college classroom. Each practice was followed by an opportunity for reflection.

The in-class content was supplemented by an instructor-developed, online, twenty-one-day mindfulness challenge, started about halfway through the semester. Given the increasing demands in their student teaching classroom, the preservice teachers and the seminar instructor were invited to commit ten to fifteen minutes a day for self-care in the form of guided daily secular mindfulness practice. The guidance was sent from the professor to each student via group text message. Preservice teachers downloaded a free meditation timer app (Insight Timer) to support their practice.

Each day, the faculty provided brief instructions for a mindfulness practice with an accompanying visual prompt. These prompts mirrored the sequence of the prior course content and gave opportunities to further practice what had been explored in the seminar sessions. The combination of narrative and visual prompts allowed for connection to different modalities.

When each meditation was completed by the student, each student replied with a text to the group indicating completion. This provided a community context for the virtual experience as well as accountability to help develop the habit of mind. While there are many ways to cultivate mindfulness, the value of both instruction and group support in developing a mindfulness practice is well documented (Epstein, 1999; McCown, Reibel, & Micozzi, 2011).

Each course meeting followed the routine of introduction of mindfulness content with links to topics related to classroom teaching, a mindfulness practice, and a written reflection. A summary of each course meeting follows.

Session 1: Introduction to Mindfulness

Content. History of secular mindfulness, summary of outcomes specific to mindfulness for teachers and students, and benefits and challenges of maintaining a mindfulness practice were introduced. Self-compassion was discussed and gratitude practice were introduced.

Link to seminar course. Preservice teachers had previously read excerpts of Carol Dweck's *Mindset: The New Psychology of Success* (2007). The concept of mind state as both malleable and integrally related to mood and behavior was discussed. The frame of considering mistakes or failures as opportunities to learn or as forms of feedback was explored.

Practice. Introduction to posture. Listening to the bell. Counting breaths.

Reflection. After taking the mindset self-assessment, reflect on your own mindset in times of challenge. How aware of your thoughts, feelings, and bodily sensations are you in times of challenge? Do you see your skills as a teacher as fixed or changeable? What is your reaction when you make mistakes or do not live up to your own performance expectations?

Session 2: Paying Attention

Content. The different ways we listen were explored. Introduced listening as an intentional activity that involves awareness of the present moment without judgment or attempts to change or control it. Discussed conversational habits that might impede deep listening (giving advice, interrupting, sharing own experience, and thinking about what you are going to say next).

Link to seminar course. Preservice teachers explored the impact of learning about and from their students through deep listening. Preservice teachers discussed ways of teaching listening skills to their elementary grade students.

Practice. Deep listening, use of labeling to lessen internal "noise."

Reflection. Write about a time when you felt truly listened to. How did you know you were being listened to? How did it feel?

Session 3: Staying in the Present

Content. Present-centered awareness was discussed. Examples of the impact of thinking about the future on anxiety and thinking about the past on wanting or regret were given. Techniques to stay in the moment were offered.

Link to seminar course. Preservice teachers discussed responses to classroom teaching evaluations and self-assessment of teaching strengths and areas for improvement. They discussed the challenge of learning from criticism without defensiveness and how worry about the future and comparison to past performance or others often shifted focus from present experience.

Practice. Returning to now. Finding your anchor (use of physical anchors including body, breath, and anchor words taught).

Reflection. Reflect on the experience of recording a daily success in the teaching day and staying with that moment.

Session 4: Listening to Your Body

Content. The value of listening to the wisdom of the body was explored. There was awareness that as external demands and constraints on time increase, the tendency to ignore or downplay physical cues supporting wellness also increases.

Link to seminar course. Preservice teachers discussed the responses of their bodies to student teaching stress, such as fatigue, increased sickness, or high irritability.

Practice. Body scan (a guided relaxation bringing attention to various parts of the body).

Reflection. When do you listen to your body? When don't you? In what ways do you care for your health and well-being during student teaching?

Session 5: Emotional Awareness

Content. The value of allowing the full range of emotion in everyday experience was discussed. The role of mindfulness in tolerating uncomfortable feelings was explained. Introduced concept of equanimity (a fully engaged calm).

Link to seminar course. Preservice teachers discussed teacher and student emotions and how they impact the classroom, and how discipline interacts with emotional expression and regulation.

Practice. Preservice teachers listened to the children's book *Moody Cow Meditates* (MacLean, 2009) and created Mind Jars—glitter globes that create a visual of allowing time and space for thoughts, bodily sensations, and emotions to settle.

Reflection. Describe a challenging moment in your teaching when you drew on mindfulness ideas or practice in response. How did it work?

Session 6: Integrating Mind, Body, and Heart in the Educational Context

Content. Mindfulness in the classroom and teaching experience were discussed.

Link to seminar course. Preservice teachers discussed places where mindfulness interfaces with their classroom, especially in creating an accepting and calm classroom tone, supporting positive behavior management, and responding to the stresses of student teaching.

Practice. Heartfulness practice/loving-kindness meditation.

Reflection. What is the value of incorporating mindfulness practice into the classroom for you and for your students? What supports and needs do you have to continue your own practice if you wish, now that you have completed the twenty-one-day challenge?

OBSERVATIONS OF A MINDFUL PRESERVICE TEACHER SEMINAR

In the seminar class, the eight preservice teachers' attention to mindfulness surfaced in a variety of ways. Verbal and written reflections described the ways participants—including the preservice teachers and the seminar instructor—responded to the variety of mindfulness activities in which they engaged.

The Power of Language

Preservice teachers began using the language of mindfulness in discussion and their writing over the semester. They described conscious efforts to breathe, to slow down time, and to settle the mind in their responses to classroom scenarios. Familiar terms such as "active listening" and "paying attention" were used in the context of mindfulness, as preservice teachers reflected on how they interacted with their students.

In journal prompts, preservice teachers described specific classroom incidents in which they were conscious of mindfulness. One preservice teacher said, "I stop for a minute and try not to react right away." Another stated, "I've been working on being able to put the distracting noise out of focus in my mind and fully pay attention to whatever student I was dealing with."

Self-affirming language appeared to become more natural to the preservice teachers as well. Preservice teachers were encouraged to record successes each day—not what happened to go well in their teaching that day but what went well that they were responsible for. Immediately following teaching, preservice teachers were to ask themselves, What did I do that I feel really good about today? What surprised me or showed me the value of my effort?

While at first the preservice teachers seemed to resist praising themselves, verbal and written reflections described an increasing willingness to do so. One preservice teacher reflected on this progression: "Although it was difficult to think of positive occurrences for each day . . . it became easier over time. I tend to focus more on what went wrong or what I could've done differently. That . . . helped me to break that habit."

Different Practices Land Differently

Differences were found in the way these preservice teachers experienced the various mindfulness activities of the seminar. The preservice teachers and instructor responded to the activities from a variety of background experiences with mindfulness. Participants identified such positive outcomes as "helped me to not get as worked up as I used to" and "helped me control my thoughts and let go or move past things that are blocking me, after I acknowledge them."

All of the participants described positive outcomes to the attention to mindfulness, but they had varying views of the effectiveness of the specific kinds of practice (such as silent meditation, guided meditation, visualization, gratitude practice, and heartfulness). While all were open to the practice and believed in its effectiveness, each needed to find the practice that best worked for them. Some students found the structure of the twenty-one-day mindfulness challenge to serve as a useful reminder to them, while others found it stressful.

Trying different ways to practice mindfulness helped reach all the students. Their ways of learning and being, preferences for information and sensory input, and prior experiences with contemplative practice were diverse. Therefore, offering different types of mindful practices and a variety of modalities to take in information increased the connection to the range of students.

It also helped mitigate the seeming hypocrisy of forced mindfulness or mindfulness as a class assignment. As mindfulness practice is a highly personal choice and journey, having it graded or required in a rigid or standard way is counterintuitive. Rather, the practices were offered as an invitation to focus on self. There was no penalty for missed or altered practice.

Student-Focused Rather than Self-Focused

In reflections on mindfulness, the preservice teachers tended to be more forthcoming about the benefits for mindfulness practice for their students than for themselves. Each described different activities with roots in mindfulness designed to help their own students pay attention to their bodies and focus throughout the school day. They noted their students engaged in yoga stretches, deep breathing, and "melting to the ground like a popsicle." The preservice teachers noted changes in their students' behavior after engaging in these activities, finding them to be calmer and more positive. For example, one stated, "I use mindfulness techniques in my classroom in order to get students calm and ready for a transition."

The preservice teachers saw the value of incorporating mindfulness into the school day for their students' benefit, but several described the challenge of finding time outside of school to engage in their own mindfulness practice. As one preservice teacher explained, "It [mindfulness practice] has stressed me out more than I know it should. By the time I'm getting home, I've been in the classroom, then gone to work or tutoring, or even the gym as well. My mind is exhausted and I still have other things to accomplish before bed, and before I know it, it's midnight."

Some preservice teachers described the impact of practicing mindfulness with their students as having a beneficial byproduct: in teaching mindfulness, they found themselves to be more relaxed and more attentive to their students. One preservice teacher commented that encouraging her students to use positive mindset language helped her as well: "I tend to focus more on what went wrong or what I could've done differently. This [experience] helped me to appreciate the positive things." The primary objective, however, appeared to be about improving their students' well-being, with their own needs secondary.

Introducing activities with a focus on the students may be a route to supporting preservice teachers' self-focus. Noting the positive effects on their students may be one means of convincing preservice teachers of the value of these activities. Frequently, teacher evaluations are tied to student performance, so logically preservice teachers focus their attention on their students over themselves.

When preservice teachers connect positive change in their students to mindfulness, they may be more open to engaging in the same practices. Additionally, underscoring the concrete benefits of mindfulness practice— that is, it supports a positive classroom climate, de-escalates behavior issues, and reduces teacher stress, which increases productivity—may convince preservice teachers of its value more effectively than general appeals to health and wellness.

BLURRING THE TEACHER-STUDENT LINES: TEACHER AS LEARNER

The co-teaching model of this project was unique. The elementary educator brought to the seminar expertise in principles of classroom instruction and assessment, while the mindfulness instruction and guidance was provided by another faculty member, who had her own mindfulness practice and experience teaching the Mindful Schools curriculum to elementary school children. Their shared interest in teacher wellness prompted the mutually beneficial collaboration.

The elementary educator had little experience with mindfulness and presented the project to the preservice teachers as a learning experience for her as well as for them. The elementary educator reflected on her own responses to the activities with the group of students, describing similar struggles in finding the time and engaging in self-compassion. This dynamic fostered a community of learners, rather than a one-way transfer of knowledge from teacher to student.

The two-professor structure of the student teaching seminar provided preservice teachers with a model of collaboration and co-teaching. In this case, the co-teaching of the seminar by faculty members with different areas of expertise mirrored the intersection between elementary education and mindfulness.

While one professor brought passion for and knowledge of mindfulness, the other brought cautious curiosity shaped by the knowledge of potential obstacles to classroom mindfulness practice. Both brought a willingness to listen and learn from one another. This experience served as a reminder that teacher educators with little experience in mindfulness can learn along with their students. The seminar became a classroom community of teachers learning from one another.

GARNERING RESOURCES AND OVERCOMING CHALLENGES

At this time, mindfulness is eliciting high interest across populations and disciplines. The evidence base of its efficacy is rapidly growing; at the same time, there is renewed interest in education about student wellness at the college level (Conley, Durlak, & Kirsch, 2015) and social emotional competencies at the K–12 level (Dymnicki, Sambolt, & Kidron, 2013). At all ages, the opportunity to reduce stress, increase engagement, and nurture self-compassion to allow a kinder, gentler, yet still productive path in life is compelling.

Despite the evidence of its value, there are obstacles to integration in preservice education. One common obstacle is time. If there is no time in the students' course load requirements for anything additional, mindfulness instruction can be embedded within existing courses rather than an additional or elective offering. Another challenge is personnel, specifically instructor expertise.

Even without extensive personal experience or expertise in mindfulness, there is much value in collaboration. Promoting partnerships in the college setting or broader community with those who have experience in mindfulness can impact the next generation of teachers. If a local collaboration is not possible, there are many virtual "teachers." Numerous mindfulness instruction options exist from texts to videos and apps. Regardless of the delivery of the instruction, teacher educators without experience in mindfulness can learn along with their students, providing an added benefit of a model in which a community of learners learn from one another, and a model of continued development and learning in a seasoned educator.

In this integration of mindfulness into a preservice teacher seminar, the language of mindfulness resonated with much of what the preservice teachers were experiencing in their elementary classrooms, from helping students pay attention to managing their own emotional reactions to stressors. Given their role and focus, much of their natural curiosity tended toward how mindfulness relates to the classroom or students.

In conclusion, while the focus on self was acknowledged as having some secondary gain (for example, being more relaxed), the motivation to learn about the role of mindfulness in teaching and its impact on students was higher than learning about how mindfulness impacted their own functioning. A future direction in integrating mindfulness in preservice teaching seminar is to build on preservice teachers' natural curiosity and comfort in learning how mindfulness impacts their students and classroom and to build their mindfulness practice from the outside in.

ESSENTIAL IDEAS TO CONSIDER

- The teaching profession is stressful. To mitigate against negative outcome, teacher self-care needs to be valued and nurtured, beginning in preservice education.
- Mindfulness practice offers a skill-based path to support teacher wellness.
- Preservice teaching seminars offer opportunities to embed mindfulness instruction and support through collaborative teaching with colleagues or community partners with training in mindfulness.
- Preservice teachers may be more motivated to practice mindfulness as part of their teaching P–12 students, benefitting both student and teacher.

REFERENCES

Caires, S., Almeida, L., & Vieira, D. (2012). Becoming a teacher: Preservice teachers' experiences and perceptions about teaching practice. *European Journal of Education, 35*(2), 163–178.

Conley, C. S., Durlak, J. A., & Kirsch, A. C. (2015). A meta-analysis of universal mental health prevention programs for higher education students. *Prevention Science, 16*(4), 487–507.

Dorman, E. (2015). Building teachers' social-emotional competence through mindful practices. *Curriculum and Teaching Dialogue, 17*(1–2), 103–119.

Dweck, C. (2007). *Mindset: The new psychology of success.* Random House.

Dymnicki, A., Sambolt, M., & Kidron, Y. (2013). *Improving college and career readiness by incorporating social and emotional learning.* Washington, DC: College and Career Readiness and Success Center at American Institutes for Research.

Epstein, R. M. (1999). Mindful practice. *JAMA, 282*(9), 833–839.

Fives, H., Hamman, D. & Olivarez, A. (2007). Does burnout begin with student teaching? Analyzing efficacy, burnout, and support during the student-teaching semester. *Teaching and Teacher Education, 23*(6), 916–934.

Flook, L., Goldberg, S. B., Pinger, L., Bonus, K., & Davidson, R. J. (2013). Mindfulness for teachers: A pilot study to assess effects on stress, burnout, and teaching efficacy. *Mind, Brain, and Education, 7*(3), 182–195.

Frank, J., Reibel, D., Broderick, P., Cantrell, T., & Metz, S. (2013). The effectiveness of mindfulness-based stress reduction on educator stress and well-being: Results from a pilot study. *Mindfulness, 4*(3), 1–9.

Gardner, S. (2010). Stress among prospective teachers: A review of the literature. *Australian Journal of Teacher Education 35*(8), 18–28.

Hanson, R. (2013). *Hardwiring happiness: The new brain science of contentment, calm, and confidence.* New York: Harmony Books.

Jennings, P. A., Frank, J. L., Snowberg, K. E., Coccia, M. A., & Greenberg, M. T. (2013). Improving classroom learning environments by Cultivating Awareness and Resilience in Education (CARE): Results of a randomized controlled trial. *School Psychology Quarterly, 28*(4), 374.

Kiken, L. G., & Shook, N. J. (2011). Looking up: Mindfulness increases positive judgments and reduces negativity bias. *Social Psychological and Personality Science, 2*(4), 425–431.

MacLean, K. L. (2009). *Moody cow meditates.* Simon & Schuster.

Malinowski, P., & Lim, H. J. (2015). Mindfulness at work: Positive affect, hope, and optimism mediate the relationship between dispositional mindfulness, work engagement, and well-being. *Mindfulness, 6*(6), 1250–1262.

McCown, D., Reibel, D., & Micozzi, M. S. (2011). *Teaching mindfulness: A practical guide for clinicians and educators.* New York: Springer.

Poulin, P. A., Mackenzie, C. S., Soloway, G., & Karayolas, E. (2008). Mindfulness training as an evidenced-based approach to reducing stress and promoting well-being among human services professionals. *International Journal of Health Promotion and Education, 46*(2), 72–80.

Roeser, R. W., Schonert-Reichl, K. A., Jha, A., Cullen, M., Wallace, L., Wilensky, R., & Harrison, J. (2013). Mindfulness training and reductions in teacher stress and burnout: Results from two randomized, waitlist-control field trials. *Journal of Educational Psychology, 105*(3), 787.

Roeser, R. W., Skinner, E., Beers, J., & Jennings, P. A. (2012). Mindfulness training and teachers' professional development: An emerging area of research and practice. *Child Development Perspectives, 6*(2), 167–173.

Rozin, P., & Royzman, E. B. (2001). Negativity bias, negativity dominance, and contagion. *Personality and Social Psychological Review, 5*(4), 296–320.

Weaver, L. & Wilding, M. (2013). *The 5 dimensions of engaged teaching: A practical guide for educators.* Bloomington, IN: Solution Tree Press.

Chapter Eight

Across Time and Space

Designing Online Contemplative Learning

Kathryn Byrnes, Bowdoin College, Brunswick, Maine

Teaching and learning require a higher degree of awareness than we ordinarily possess—and awareness is always heightened when we are caught in a creative tension. Paradox is another name for that tension, a way of holding opposites together that creates an electric charge that keeps us awake.
——Parker Palmer (1998, pp. 73–74)

Contemplative[1] pedagogy consists of "educational practices which reveal, clarify and make manifest the nature of the reality of one's mind, the minds of others, the world, and the relationships among all three" (Byrnes & Bassarear, 2015, p. 34). Contemplative pedagogy is not limited to face-to-face, synchronous learning. Many teacher educators, myself included, are expanding our pedagogy into online and hybrid forms. This shift requires "a higher degree of awareness," as Parker Palmer notes above, of the creative tensions or paradoxes facing teaching and learning across time and space.

Designing contemplative online contemplative learning environments for preservice and in-service educators[2] offers several challenges that require skillful management of technology, people, time, and resources. Challenges of teacher education in general include limited time for professional development, difficulty transitioning between roles as a teacher and roles as a learner, and substantial knowledge, practice, and reflection required for effectiveness.

Challenges of online teacher education include unrestricted time for communication and assignments that can lead to feeling overwhelmed; a distanced perspective without face-to-face contact that can lead to misunder-

standing or isolation; and the requirement of substantial knowledge and experience with technology. In both contexts, teacher educators face the challenges of creating learning environments that build on students' prior knowledge and experience, enhance cultural awareness, and develop pedagogical
content knowledge and competence.

Palmer, a writer, activist, and educator, outlined six paradoxical tensions
he found contributing to the pedagogical design of his university teaching in
his seminal 1998 text *The Courage to Teach: Exploring the Inner Landscape
of a Teacher's Life*. Paradoxes are seemingly opposites, yet are connected
and complementary. Palmer (1998) advocates, "If we want to know what is
essential, we must stop thinking the world into pieces and start thinking it
together again" (p. 63).

It is crucial to understand that paradoxes are not problems to be solved.
They are tensions to be managed. Instead of creating either/or, dichotomous
choices, paradoxes should be open to a both/and perspective. The six tensions are as follows:

1. The space should be bounded and open.
2. The space should be hospitable and "charged."
3. The space should invite the voice of the individual and the voice of the
   group.
4. The space should honor the "little" stories of the students and the
   "big" stories of the disciplines and tradition.
5. The space should support solitude and surround it with the resources
   of community.
6. The space should welcome both silence and speech. (Palmer, 1998, p.
   74)

While Palmer was referring to a physical classroom space, these six paradoxes equally apply to contemplative online learning environments. Throughout
this chapter, each paradox will be analyzed with examples shared from a
hybrid, graduate, for-credit course offered in the summer of 2016 titled
Mindful Education. While the course was unique in many respects, the paradoxes of teaching and learning and the lessons gleaned from this course may
apply to other contemplative online classes.

The course operated for twelve weeks and consisted of eight graduate
students and the professor. Students worked as educators in every level of
education from early childhood through higher education, and many were
interested in transitioning to becoming mindfulness educators in their local
schools, districts, or states. In the course, educators cultivated the knowledge
and skills to integrate mindfulness-based best practices into curricula, classrooms, and other pre–K through university educational settings.

The course included critical examination of mindful education literature and research, and opportunities for independent projects and small-group collaboration. Course participants investigated topics central to the field such as social-emotional development, the neurobiology of mindfulness, self-care, and mindful movement. The course learning objectives were as follows:

- critically examine what constitutes a mindful education;
- assess how mindful learning and teaching can be integrated into diverse educational settings;
- analyze the cultural appropriateness of mindful practices with diverse educational populations;
- critique multiple models of mindful educational programs; and
- design mindful lessons appropriate to specific educational contexts.

Each week or module (Monday to Sunday) consisted of a focused topic, learning objectives, a brief description, and a list of the course materials including video, audio, articles, and book chapters, a mindful practice exploration, and learning assignments. In learning communities of four course participants, students posted discussions about the course materials, building on their understandings and questions from previous weeks. Learning assignments served as formative assessments building toward their final project of presenting what they learned about mindful education to a local audience of their choosing.

Students lived in two states on the East Coast of the United States, and the instructor lived on the West Coast. Many students traveled within the United States and abroad as part of their personal summer travel during the twelve weeks; with the asynchronous nature of the course, we were able to be engaged at any time and any place. A five-day residency occurred halfway through the course. The three in-person class sessions during residency had a huge impact on the class dynamic and the formation of a community of learners rather than just a group of classmates.

The Mindful Education course was similar to a course taught previously in a traditional college classroom with undergraduate teacher education students (Byrnes & Bassarear, 2015; Byrnes & Caron, 2017). In some ways having an existing face-to-face course to adapt to an online format can be helpful; it can also be limiting. No automatic translation exists from face-to-face to online learning. Space and time offer new paradoxes to hold and new constraints and opportunities to consider. The following sections explicate these paradoxes for online contemplative teacher education.

BOUNDED AND OPEN

While faculty may be full time or adjunct, located in the same place as the university or at a distance, and working with preservice or in-service educators, all instructors teaching online face the constraints of the university and available technology in their course design. Teacher educators are well versed in pedagogical content knowledge, knowledge of curricula, and knowledge of learning contexts as prerequisite knowledge for practicing teachers (Shulman, 1986).

As of 2009, TPACK, or technology, pedagogy, and content knowledge, is specialized knowledge required by educators and teacher educators (Koehler & Mishra, 2009). Matthew Koehler and Punya Mishra (2009) include both analog and digital, as well as new and old, technologies in their definition of technology, acknowledging that most technologies in use and being studied are newer and digital. They argue that the integration of content, pedagogy, and technology "produces the types of flexible knowledge needed to successfully integrate technology use into teaching" (p. 60).

The structure or boundaries of a course and technology create the openness and flexibility that are essential for contemplative learning environments. Too many boundaries with course materials or assignments stifle the openness and flexibility needed for contemplative learning. Some of the considerations for boundaries within online contemplative learning environments include the type and amount of course materials and assignments. Too much or too little of either denies the "electric charge that keeps us awake," as Palmer referenced in the opening quotation.

For example, I often assign too much reading in courses. This ineffective design occurs because I love to read and value students being exposed to a range of diverse, stimulating course materials in the short time we have together. By recognizing this bias in my design through reflection and feedback on prior course evaluations, and being open and flexible enough to adapt, students now experience an enhanced learning environment with fewer and more carefully curated course materials.

Some universities offer courses for faculty to learn about teaching and learning online. This kind of preparation can be invaluable for teacher educators understanding how to structure a course with clear, appropriate expectations for assignments and learning activities. I had the privilege to work with multiple instructional designers on the Mindful Education course who offered clear suggestions about scaffolding for assignments, enhanced clarity for assignment descriptions and rubrics, and technological tools for assignments involving multiple sources of data.

For our collaboration to be effective it was crucial for me to embrace my discomfort with what I didn't know about TPACK and be confident in my pedagogical content knowledge, as well as knowledge of curricula and learning contexts. My TPACK was greatly enhanced through the collaboration with instructional designers and a required course that both modeled and taught how to teach online.

The required course was completed with five other faculty prior to designing Mindful Education. I also took an online class as a student to gain insight into the online student's experience, and this greatly enhanced my appreciation of the openness that arises through appropriate, clearly communicated boundaries. The bounded and open paradox adheres to the Goldilocks principle: not too much, not too little, just right. Consciously designing course materials and assignments with this intention supports a bounded and open learning space.

HOSPITABLE AND "CHARGED"

Wow, I am energized by the discussion this week. It feels very real to take a resource from this class and apply it to our work.

—Carol,[3] July 2016

The paradox of unlimited time for students and the instructor is even more challenging in an online learning environment. When dialogue can happen 24-7, it can be difficult to create a hospitable and "charged" learning context. Students can post on discussion boards, blogs, or wikis anytime day or night, which means that hours or days can pass with little to no discussion or lots of discussion can happen in a short time. The structure for the dialogue guides the course participants to feel invited to contribute. In the Mindful Education course, the following paragraph in the syllabus delineated the expectations for online discussion:

> The majority of our communication will occur online. Here are some guidelines to foster learning, respectful dialogue, and inquiry. They are adapted from the Center for Courage and Renewal (http://www.couragerenewal.org).

- Presume welcome and extend welcome.
- Be as present as possible for ourselves and others.
- Seek to understand before you seek to be understood.
- Speak your truth in ways that respect other people's truth.
- When the going gets rough, turn to wonder.

These guidelines apply to both in-person and online communication. As an instructor, they serve as guideposts for communication with students. This means responding within a day, if possible, to questions, regularly reading and responding to comments and discussions, and modeling all of these guidelines in every form of communication. I scheduled to check the course website once per day for new contributions. Responding to discussion posts within a few days or at least once per week, responding to assignments within a week, and responding to e-mails or questions daily became my norm.

A challenge both for instructors and students is feeling as if communication should be instant and that you are always engaged in the course. Laura Douglass (2007) observed the following about online communication and her attitude toward technology: "If I sit down to answer a threaded discussion and hope to get it done quickly due to not wanting to be on the computer, the lack of contemplation will be reflected in my answers and negatively affect the student's own experience of online learning, as well as his or her own relationship with technology" (p. 2). Acknowledging our state of mind and intention as instructors is crucial for communicating effectively with compassion and mindfulness. Supporting a hospitable and "charged" climate for learning online does not require unlimited time and resources but does require consistent, habitual, compassionate communication behaviors.

VOICE OF THE INDIVIDUAL AND GROUP

You know what, Armando, I think you may be convincing me to read this article again.
                                                        —Arlie, August 2016

As an instructor, part of the role is to support, encourage, and sometimes provoke deeper levels of understanding through questions or observations. To skillfully allow students to share their understandings and misunderstandings requires detailed, compassionate attention. Palmer (1998) observed, "The teacher's task is to listen for what the group voice is saying and to play that voice back from time to time so the group can hear and even change its own collective mind" (pp. 75–76).

Moderating or facilitating a discussion is quite different from leading a discussion. Depending on the course participants, an online instructor may need to employ different tools. For example, with a group of graduate students who are also educators, my role was very much to facilitate more than lead. I often responded to learning community conversations at the end of a week and highlighted key ideas that were presented, themes I observed in the conversation, and anything new I had to contribute. Here is one example from halfway through the course:

> Hello. I think Ryen said it best when she observed how energizing the conversation was this week. 7/8 members of the class commented! I am so humbled and amazed by the capacity to take a resource like a reading or video and immediately make it applicable to your work like Ayesha did with the STEM

professional development. The wealth of insights grappled with in your discussion is powerful and reflects such transformative learning for me.

It is so important to recognize that a lot of resistance from educators may stem from feeling powerless with all the mandates they are expected to do without great professional development or support to make it happen and often coming from people with little to no experience in classrooms working with students. Mindfulness in education can easily feel like a fad or one more thing to do, which is a reasonable response based on their past experiences. Thank you for acknowledging and exploring the issue of adult and student resistance in your conversation.

In this feedback, students received highlights of their conversation, insight into teacher resistance, and appreciation for the application of course materials to their work as educators from the professor. While some students commented in a midcourse evaluation that they wanted more definitive comments by the professor on key ideas from the course materials, others recognized that the professor is not the sole authority on the topic.

The course was designed as a community of learners model rather than a transmission model of teaching and learning, a perspective that guided my contributions to the online discussions. In a community-of-learners model articulated by Barbara Rogoff (1994), "students learn the information as they collaborate with other 'children' and with adults in carrying out activities with purposes connected explicitly with the history and current practices of the community" (p. 211). Rather than being student led or teacher led, communities of learners engage in teacher-to-student, student-to-teacher, and student-to-student learning with similar rigor and frequency.

As one example of student-to-student learning, in the last week of the course, one reading was particularly dense and philosophical, leading to varying challenges for students. One of the last comments in the learning community discussion forum was, "You know what, Armando, I think you may be convincing me to read this article again." This acknowledgment by one individual reflects the openness students brought to learning from each other.

Students built on each other's observations and insights and were encouraged to rethink or reconsider a particular viewpoint or perspective based on a colleague's insight. This capacity to authentically share as an individual can be enhanced through the collective voice of the group particularly because of the permanent nature of conversations online, which can be reread and expanded at any time.

HONOR "LITTLE" STORIES OF THE STUDENTS AND "BIG" STORIES OF THE DISCIPLINES AND TRADITION

Palmer (1998) explains that this fourth paradox is one of the most difficult to hold as an instructor. "It is a hard tension to hold—not only because academia discredits the little story but also because the little stories are the ones students feel most comfortable with. Given free rein, they will hide out in their little stories and evade the big ones" (p. 80).

Respectful communication, open invitations for reflection and analysis, and course materials and assignments relevant to students' work becoming educators allow the individual stories of students and the collective stories of the teaching profession to coexist in a symbiotic relationship. Within a teacher education course integrating contemplation, first-person experiences with contemplative practices are essential.

In the Mindful Education course, students practiced a different contemplative practice each week, chose a personal contemplative practice for twenty-one days, and journaled about all of these experiences. The journals were open to everyone in the class as a way to enhance our understanding of the challenges and insights all students experienced as individuals. The recommended format for journals included the following:

- Date, name of the practice, and time spent practicing;
- Three words to describe the experience; and
- Bullet points or pictures explaining any insights, observations, or questions that arose.

As much as possible, students described the experience in detail before moving into any analysis or sensemaking process. Staying close to the experience allows for meaningful, honest, and open insights, observations, and questions to occur. The insights shared often developed from a student's background or prior experiences. In addition, analysis and sensemaking integrate first-person experience with the contemplative practice; second-person dialogue with other students, mentors, teachers, family members, or friends; and third-person resources such as course materials.

The twenty-one-day practice concluded with a reflection paper on the contemplative practice experienced throughout the course, and these papers were available to all students. Without dialogue/second-person understandings, and connection to relevant texts/third-person understandings, first-person experiences remain rooted in the little stories of the individual.

The following student log reveals the complementarity of third- and first-person learning experiences while experimenting with Joseph Goldstein's (2013) guided emotional awareness contemplative practice. Sasha connects her personal contemplative experience with the big story of emotional awareness as described by Goldstein:

> A sudden insight! "Awareness has the capacity to be with whatever arises" — Goldstein. I spent a few minutes scrolling back through the video to find these exact words. As I said them aloud, my boyfriend came over and dumped a pile of clean laundry on me. "Show me your capacity!" he joked. When I heard Goldstein's words, thinking seemed to cease as I felt the meaning in my body. Practicing emotional awareness has helped me to better notice and distinguish amongst a variety of emotions.
>
> This practice has taken away some of the self-criticism and judgment around my inner feelings; I have trained myself to just notice, rather than judge harshly or try to stop them. I also feel less reactive in situations (although this may have to do with the decreased workload in summertime). Overall, I feel further intrigued by the practice. I am also grateful for the space and time to actually carry out the practice.

This mindfulness journal entry as well as so many others served as inspiration for reflection, inquiry, and connection for all students and the professor. Utilizing technology to make students' work accessible to all course participants not only increases the quality of the work due to the enhanced accountability; it also demonstrates an emphasis on student-to-student learning. Clear expectations for assignments, modeling, and direct feedback on student work invites a perspective of honor for both the little stories of the individual and the big stories of the discipline.

SUPPORT SOLITUDE AND SURROUND IT WITH THE RESOURCES OF COMMUNITY

Let him who cannot be alone beware of community. Let him who is not in community beware of being alone. Each by itself has profound perils and pitfalls. One who wants fellowship without solitude plunges into the void of words and feelings, and the one who seeks solitude without fellowship perishes in the abyss of vanity, self-infatuation and despair.

—Dietrich Bonhoeffer (1954, p. 77)

Linda Watts (2014), a professor in the School of Interdisciplinary Arts and Sciences at the University of Washington, Bothell, observed two powerful insights after designing and teaching online: "(1) that in some instances, and in some respects, online learning might prove preferable to (not merely as good as) face-to-face instruction; and (2) that mindfulness education might achieve certain nuances and felicities only through online environments."

Online learning occurs typically in solitude for students. Whether students are part of a cohort or taking courses ad hoc, they regularly are not in physical contact with any of their classmates or instructor. Often in face-to-face learning, solitude is not as easily attained, which can be a detriment to many students. Supporting solitude and surrounding it with the resources of community may be more possible through online learning.

In the Mindful Education course, seven of the eight students were part of a master's degree cohort in mindfulness studies. Some were in their first year of the program and some in the second. One student was pursuing his PhD and not part of the cohort model. While the majority of the students lived in one metropolitan area, they did not discuss physically getting together to work on the course besides the required residency at the midpoint of the course.

Students shared going individually to libraries, coffee shops, offices, and home office spaces to do the course work. Some students worked in the early morning, others during kids' naptimes, and others late at night. Many experienced challenges in their everyday lives to create solitude and space to think about course materials and practice mindfulness, but all managed to create the solitude they needed for learning. One student even shared that she pretended to sleep while traveling with her family to practice metta (loving-kindness or friendly wishes) meditation without being interrupted.

Learning purely in solitude can lead to disconnection and decrease motivation in some students. Being accountable to a small group with a project and making discussions and assignments public for the whole class help to support individual learning with the resources of a community. In the Mindful Education course, students collaborated on an in-class presentation that occurred during the in-person residency and learning community discussions. In addition, student submissions for all of the assignments were available for review by all the classmates and professor on the Blackboard website.

A few assignments required peer review, but students could comment and learn from each other on every assignment submitted. Students engaged in mindfulness practices as individuals. Written reflections on those experiences created a wider base of knowledge beyond one's personal experience. Student contributions and engagement are compulsory to create a community of learners. The role of the instructor included modeling, supporting, and coaxing those student contributions.

WELCOME SILENCE AND SPEECH

Seeking to nurture, to educate, to inspire, silence in educational settings may reach places that speech can, at best, only evoke. The difficulty is first to identify and call attention to the various kinds of silence in the public context of the classroom and then to create spaces that nurture, challenge, or enrich these silences.

—Michalinos Zembylas and Pavlos Michaelides (2004, p. 203)

Silence is generally a key component of contemplative practice. For many, practicing contemplation in silence allows the skills of attention, emotional awareness and regulation, and compassion/kindness to be cultivated away from the stress and challenges of daily life. "Pausing during teaching is not easy to learn, but practicing silence and stillness in our daily meditation practice can give us the experience and the courage to pause before responding in a classroom setting" (Brown, 2011, p. 81). Once those skills have been developed, they become more likely to transfer to daily living.

Silence often takes the form of wait time or silence after a question has been asked by a teacher or after a student responds to a teacher's question. Early research by Dr. Mary Budd Rowe (1986) revealed that wait time is often less than one second, while the optimal time is closer to three to five seconds. In teacher education, preservice teachers learn about wait time and yet too often don't experience it being modeled by teacher educators. Wait time can elicit an empty mind, a busy mind, discomfort, or reflection for students and educators. What distinguishes contemplative wait time is the presence of the learners and the teacher.

In an online asynchronous course, wait time occurs all the time. Instead of seconds, wait time can be minutes, hours, or days. The space in conversations and the public, more permanent nature of written dialogue invites more carefully considered speech. While pauses and silence can frequently occur in online conversations, it is still centrally important that students and educators create time for silence in the teaching and learning process.

According to the Quaker tradition, silence allows individuals to gain access to inner resources and wisdom. "Through sitting in silence, students learn about their inner resources, at the same time affirming their connection to the community" (Schultz, 2009, p. 75). The lack of silence limits the capacity of students and teachers. Too much speech does not allow students to access "places that speech can, at best, only evoke" as Zembylas and Michaelides observed above.

Pauses or silence in one's speech, within dialogue with others, or while reading a text, watching a film, or listening to a guided audio create opportunities to stay present in the moment by being aware of one's thoughts, feelings, and physical sensations. Present-centered awareness welcomes both silence and speech.

CONCLUSION

John Davis (2006), a professor and director at Naropa University, posited, "I wasn't sure we could teach online in student-oriented ways, in a human-centered way, and in an inspired and inspiring way" (p. 28). Naropa University is the only contemplative university in North America and a pioneer in online contemplative education. In 2004 and 2006 they documented two panel presentations exploring best practices in online contemplative education. The insights shared by the faculty in this document signify early understandings and misunderstandings about online and hybrid forms of contemplative teaching and learning.

Palmer's insights about the six tensions faced in his higher education classes offer teacher educators a useful framework for designing and implementing online contemplative teacher education courses that match Davis's description above. Each of the six tensions support the others and are essential to effectively manage space and time for teacher education students. The following reviews the six tensions and the complementary contemplative pedagogy.

ESSENTIAL IDEAS TO CONSIDER

- Following the Goldilocks principle (not too much, not too little, just right) for course materials and assignments creates bounded and open spaces.
- Communicating with compassion and mindfulness by setting and enforcing clear communication expectations and methods allows for hospitable and "charged" spaces.
- Creating a community of learners who regularly engage in teacher-to-student, student-to-teacher, and student-to-student learning invites the voice of the individual and the voice of the group.
- Integrating first-person experiences with contemplative practices, second-person dialogue about the experiences, and third-person connection to theory and research honors the "little" stories of the students and the "big" stories of the disciplines and tradition.
- Cultivating intrapersonal and interpersonal skills through individual and group assignments supports solitude and surrounds it with the resources of community.
- Remaining present in the moment through wait time welcomes both silence and speech.

NOTES

1. Throughout the chapter, I will use the terms *contemplative* and *mindfulness* interchangeably.

2. The terms *teacher* and *educator* will be used interchangeably throughout the chapter. *Educator* is a more broadly inclusive term, while *teacher* often refers to one who works in a classroom setting.

3. All names of students have been changed.

REFERENCES

Bonhoeffer, D. (1954). *Life together: The classic exploration of faith in community*. New York: HarperOne.

Brown, R. (2011). The mindful teacher as the foundation of contemplative pedagogy. In J. Simmer-Brown & F. Grace (Eds.), *Meditation and the classroom: Contemplative pedagogy for religious studies* (pp. 75–83). Albany, NY: SUNY Press.

Byrnes, K., & Bassarear, T. (2015). Enhancing learning through contemplative pedagogy. In K. Ragoonaden (Ed.), *Mindful teaching and learning: Developing a pedagogy of well-being* (pp. 33–47). Lanham, MD: Lexington Books.

Byrnes, K., & Caron, J. (2017). Mindfulness in education: Contemplative inquiry in a community of learners. In O. Gunnlaugson, C. Scott, H. Bai, & E. W. Sarath (Eds.), *The intersubjective turn: Theoretical approaches to contemplative learning and inquiry across disciplines*. Albany, NY: SUNY Press.

Davis, J. (2006). Critical thinking, experiential education, and contemplative education online. In Best practices in online contemplative education: Naropa online faculty panel discussions. Retrieved from http://naropa.edu.

Douglass, L. (2007). Contemplative online learning environments. *Journal of Online Education (JOE)*. Retrieved from http://www.nyu.edu.

Goldstein, J. (2013, April 27). Guided meditation on emotions. YouTube. Retrieved from https://www.youtube.com.

Koehler, M. J., & Mishra, P. (2009). What is technological pedagogical content knowledge? *Contemporary Issues in Technology and Teacher Education, 9*(1), 60–70.

Palmer, P. J. (1998). *The courage to teach: Exploring the inner landscape of a teacher's life*. San Francisco, CA: Jossey-Bass.

Rogoff, B. (1994). Developing understanding of the idea of communities of learners. *Mind, Culture, and Activity, 1*(4), 209–229.

Rowe, M. B. (1986). Wait time: Slowing down may be a way of speeding up! *Journal of Teacher Education, 37*(1), 43–50.

Schultz, K. (2009). *Rethinking classroom participation: Listening to silent voices*. New York: Teachers College Press.

Shulman, L. S. (1986). Those who understand: Knowledge growth in teaching. *Educational Researcher, 15*(2), 4–14.

Watts, L. (2014, October 7). Mindfulness in higher education. Center for Teaching and Learning, University of Washington. Retrieved from http://www.washington.edu.

Zembylas, M., & Michaelides, P. (2004). The sound of silence in pedagogy. *Educational Theory, 54*(2), 193–210.

Appendix

GOALS AND OBJECTIVES: MIDDLE CHILDHOOD SOCIAL STUDIES EDUCATION METHODS COURSE FROM CHAPTER 5

Teacher candidates will:

1. Develop a working understanding of foundational principles and objectives of middle childhood social studies education in the twenty-first century:

   a. Examine interdisciplinary approaches to social studies by considering multiple perspectives on local, national, and global issues.
   b. Examine various themes found in the Ohio social studies standards, as well as common core reading and writing standards for social studies.
   c. Examine and incorporate use of technology.
   d. Incorporate the four C's of twenty-first century learning: communication, collaboration, critical thinking, and creativity into lesson planning.

2. Apply theories, concepts, and strategies learned and observed throughout the course to design and teach lesson plans that are engaging, culturally responsive, and student centered:

   a. Teach in culturally responsive ways, which recognizes student's cultural, linguistic, and ability backgrounds.
   b. Incorporate issues of diversity into lesson planning to meet needs of students from diverse backgrounds and with varying needs, interests, and learning styles.

c. Identify and practice a variety of instructional methods and strategies for teaching social studies, which are appropriate for middle childhood students.

3. Develop strategies for incorporating student experiences and interests in and out of school into lessons that foster a student-centered, culturally relevant, and safe learning environment:

a. Write reflections and lesson plans that incorporate local and global perspectives through the use of primary and secondary sources, technologies, and media.
b. Design lesson plans that include state and national content standards, essential question(s), and skill and conceptual development related to lesson topics.
c. Design a lesson sequence on a topic taught in a middle childhood social studies class that includes lessons, resources, materials, student-centered use of technology, and an assessment:

   i. Lesson plans will include measureable learning objectives and assessments that align with those objectives, specific procedures to be followed by the teacher, specific questions to be asked of students, checks for student understanding, student-centered learning opportunities, and opportunities for students to demonstrate learning.

4. Develop perspective consciousness through discussion and assignments that incorporate multiple perspectives, diverse resources, and various technologies:

a. Locate, discuss, and evaluate social studies teaching resources.
b. Employ course readings, experiences, and independent research when contributing to discussions in class and in an online setting around issues in social studies education.
c. Facilitate online and in-class discussions that draw upon theory and practice observed and discussed during students' experiences in various classroom settings.
d. Integrate concepts of global education to better understand the complexity of current issues on local, national, and global levels.

5. Develop habits of the mind and heart in order to challenge self and others to learn new ideas and concepts regarding issues found in middle childhood social studies education, with emphasis on issues of equity and diversity, global issues, various cultures, and multiple perspectives:

a. Write reflections that incorporate individual analysis, evaluation of resources, and/or lesson ideas to be used in a middle childhood classroom.

b. Participate in formal and informal discussions that require one to cite evidence to support and refute claims made by authors and classmates, as well as collaborate to solve rather than simply identify problems.

c. Use reflective techniques to improve teaching and learning.

d. Facilitate online and in-class discussions that draw upon theory and practice observed and discussed during students' experiences in various classroom settings.

Index

About the Editors and Contributors

Kathryn Byrnes, PhD, is the Baldwin Program Director in the Center for Learning and Teaching at Bowdoin College, and faculty member at the Teachings in Mindful Education (TiME) Institute in Maine. She served as board president of the Mindfulness in Education Network (MiEN), and taught in-person and online courses on Mindful Education at Lesley University and Bowdoin College. Her scholarship and professional development work focuses on the integration of contemplative pedagogy in educational contexts.

Jane E. Dalton, PhD, is assistant professor of art education at the University of North Carolina at Charlotte teaching art education and studio art. Her research interests include arts-based learning, transformative learning, and contemplative practices to promote embodied learning. A textile artist, Jane's work has been exhibited throughout the United States. She is the coauthor of *The Compassionate Classroom: Lessons that Nurture Empathy and Wisdom* and author of the blog *The Expressive Teacher* (http://theexpressiveteacher.com).

Elizabeth Hope Dorman, PhD, is associate professor of teacher education at Fort Lewis College, in Durango, Colorado, where she teaches graduate and undergraduate students in secondary, K–12, elementary education, and teacher leadership programs. Her research interests include the integration and effects of mindfulness and contemplative practices and pedagogies on teacher development of social-emotional competence, particularly in diverse contexts and courses that address multicultural perspectives and equity issues.

* * *

Tami Augustine is clinical assistant professor of social studies and middle childhood education in the Department of Teaching and Learning at the Ohio State University. Her research interests include social studies teacher education, the intersection of spiritual pedagogy and critical global education, and contemplative practices in teaching and learning. She is coeditor and chapter author of a book entitled *Research in Global Citizenship Education.*

Heather Bandeen is assistant professor with the Advanced Degree and Administrative Licensure Department in the School of Education at Hamline University in St. Paul, Minnesota. She also serves as co-coordinator of Minnesota's Education Policy Fellowship Program. Prior to this work, she was an education faculty member at Inver Hills Community College.

Katie Egan Cunningham is associate professor at Manhattanville College in the literacy department. She is the author of *Story: Still the Heart of Literacy Learning* (2015), coauthor of *Literacy Leadership in Changing Schools: Ten Keys to Successful Professional Development* (2016), and coauthor of the popular blog *The Classroom Bookshelf.* Her research, scholarship, and teaching focuses on children's literature, new technologies, literacy methods, professional development, and intentional teaching toward student and teacher happiness.

Maureen Hall, PhD, is associate professor of education at the University of Massachusetts Dartmouth. As a teacher educator, she studies the role of literacy, mindfulness, and service learning for the holistic development, well-being, and deepened learning of students and teachers. Her scholarship is marked by compassion and a sense of belief in the need for teachers to connect in significant ways with students.

Elizabeth G. Holtzman is a licensed psychologist and associate professor of school psychology at Rhode Island College. She describes developing a mindfulness practice as the smartest choice she keeps making. In her work, Elizabeth gets to share mindfulness with students from pre-K through graduate school. She is eternally grateful for the teachers and the community of Mindful Schools for the guidance, support, and passion inspired in her personal mindfulness journey.

Libby Falk Jones, PhD, is a writer and professor of English at Berea College in Berea, Kentucky, where she holds the Chester D. Tripp Chair in Humanities. She teaches a variety of writing courses, including creative writing, journalism, technical communication, and experimental writing. Founding director of Berea's Learning Center, she has written on faculty development, contemplative pedagogies, and the teaching of writing.

Mary-Ann Mitchell-Pellett has been engaged in learner-centered and arts-inspired education as a public school educator (teacher, counselor, and school-based administrator) and more recently as an instructor in the undergraduate and graduate programs at the University of Calgary Werklund School of Education. Her research interests include reflective and contemplative practices for students, teachers, and leaders; inclusive education; narrative therapy utilizing digital storytelling; and design thinking to support social innovation and change.

Carolyn H. Obel-Omia is assistant professor of elementary education at Rhode Island College. Her career has been guided by a passion for developing a love of reading and writing in students from preschool through college. Her elementary school teaching experience includes classroom teaching in public, charter, and independent elementary schools. At the college level, she teaches literacy methods courses to elementary and early childhood teacher candidates.

Aminda J. O'Hare, PhD, is assistant professor of psychology at the University of Massachusetts Dartmouth. O'Hare studies the neural mechanisms of attention and emotion interactions. She has received training in Mindfulness-Based Stress Reduction and has started using this training to examine how attention and emotion interactions change with mindfulness practice.

Jeremy Forest Price is assistant professor of technology, innovation, and pedagogy in urban education at Indiana University–Purdue University Indianapolis. Price's research and teaching focus on supporting the development of purposeful practices based on critical reflection with technology to support good and just teaching by preservice and in-service teachers.

Kristin N. Rainville is assistant professor in the Department of Educational Leadership and Literacy at the Isabelle Farrington College of Education at Sacred Heart University in Fairfield, Connecticut. Kristin is a former classroom teacher, literacy coach, and coordinator of the Office of Early Literacy for the New Jersey Department of Education.